Smoking Cessation V   evention

Smoking Cessation With Weight Gain Prevention

A GROUP PROGRAM

Workbook

Bonnie Spring

OXFORD
UNIVERSITY PRESS

2009

OXFORD
UNIVERSITY PRESS

Oxford University Press, Inc., publishes works that further
Oxford University's objective of excellence
in research, scholarship, and education.

Oxford   New York
Auckland   Cape Town   Dar es Salaam   Hong Kong   Karachi
Kuala Lumpur   Madrid   Melbourne   Mexico City   Nairobi
New Delhi   Shanghai   Taipei   Toronto

With offices in
Argentina   Austria   Brazil   Chile   Czech Republic   France   Greece
Guatemala   Hungary   Italy   Japan   Poland   Portugal   Singapore
South Korea   Switzerland   Thailand   Turkey   Ukraine   Vietnam

Copyright © 2009 by Oxford University Press, Inc.

Published by Oxford University Press, Inc.
198 Madison Avenue, New York, New York 10016

www.oup.com

Oxford is a registered trademark of Oxford University Press

ISBN-978-0-19-531400-7 Paper

9 8 7 6 5 4 3 2 1

Printed in the United States of America
on acid-free paper

About Treatments *ThatWork*™

One of the most difficult problems confronting patients with various disorders and diseases is finding the best help available. Everyone is aware of friends or family who have sought treatment from a seemingly reputable practitioner, only to find out later from another doctor that the original diagnosis was wrong or the treatments recommended were inappropriate or perhaps even harmful. Most patients, or family members, address this problem by reading everything they can about their symptoms, seeking out information on the Internet, or aggressively "asking around" to tap knowledge from friends and acquaintances. Governments and healthcare policymakers are also aware that people in need do not always get the best treatments—something they refer to as "variability in healthcare practices."

Now healthcare systems around the world are attempting to correct this variability by introducing "evidence-based practice." This simply means that it is in everyone's interest that patients get the most up-to-date and effective care for a particular problem. Healthcare policymakers have also recognized that it is very useful to give consumers of healthcare as much information as possible, so that they can make intelligent decisions in a collaborative effort to improve physical and mental health. This series, Treatments *ThatWork*™, is designed to accomplish just that. Only the latest and most effective interventions for particular problems are described in user-friendly language. To be included in this series, each treatment program must pass the highest standards of evidence available, as determined by a scientific advisory board. Thus, when individuals suffering from these problems or their family members seek out an expert clinician who is familiar with these interventions and decides that they are appropriate, they will have confidence that they are receiving the best care available. Of course, only your health care professional can decide on the right mix of treatments for you.

This workbook is designed for your use as you participate in the smoking cessation group program. Over the course of 16 weeks, you will learn how to successfully quit smoking without gaining weight. However, the most important health goal is the cessation of smoking. Issues of weight are addressed secondarily. This is **not** a diet plan.

You will begin the quit process by gradually decreasing the number of cigarettes you smoke each day. As you taper the number of your cigarettes, you will learn how to successfully manage your withdrawal symptoms and urges to smoke. Coping skills will help you deal with high-risk situations and relapse prevention planning. Halfway through the program, you will begin managing your weight through the use of a meal replacement program. Your group leader will work with you to choose an appropriate meal plan. You will also participate in group walks as a way to improve your physical fitness. The objective of this program is to help you quit smoking altogether and improve your overall health and quality of life.

David H. Barlow, Editor-in-Chief,
Treatments *ThatWork*™
Boston, MA

Acknowledgments

Development of this treatment was supported in part by National Institutes of Health grant HL075451 and by an award from the American Cancer Society. I would like to acknowledge the editorial help of Mariclaire Cloutier and Cristina Wojdylo of Oxford University Press.

Contents

Chapter 1   Welcome   *1*

Chapter 2   Getting Started   *3*

Chapter 3   Session 1   *11*

Chapter 4   Session 2   *19*

Chapter 5   Session 3   *25*

Chapter 6   Session 4   *29*

Chapter 7   Session 5   *33*

Chapter 8   Session 6   *39*

Chapter 9   Session 7   *47*

Chapter 10   Session 8   *55*

Chapter 11   Session 9   *61*

Chapter 12   Session 10   *65*

Chapter 13   Session 11   *67*

Chapter 14   Session 12   *71*

Chapter 15   Session 13   *75*

Chapter 16   Session 14   *79*

Chapter 17   Session 15   *85*

Chapter 18   Session 16   *95*

                 Appendix of Forms   *99*

Chapter 1 *Welcome*

Congratulations on your decision to quit smoking! Cigarette smoking is the single most preventable cause of death in the United States. Each year, smoking claims the lives of 440,000 adults either through cancer, heart disease, or stroke.

Many people, women in particular, fear that quitting smoking will lead to weight gain. Although a weight gain of between 5 and 10 pounds during the first few months of cessation is normal, there are things you can do to maintain your weight.

This group program is designed to help you quit smoking without gaining weight. However, the **first** and **most important** goal is the cessation of smoking. That is the focus of the group and the most important health goal.

Over the course of the next 16 weeks, you will learn the skills and acquire the tools you need to understand and break your smoking habit. You will work together with the other members of your group, providing each other with support and encouragement. Your group leader will help you design a plan for quitting that involves tapering or gradually reducing the number of cigarettes you smoke per day until you are completely smoke-free. Once you have succeeded in eliminating your smoking habit, you will then focus on maintaining your current weight. It is important to remember, however, that this is **not** a weight-loss program. It is program for smokers who want to quit without experiencing associated weight gain and slowed metabolism.

During the weight maintenance phase of the program, you will be introduced to a meal replacement program designed specifically for you. Together with your group leader you will determine your body's daily calorie needs and you will purchase healthy foods (either online or at the grocery store) that allow you to stay within your target calorie range. You will also begin incorporating physical activity into your daily routine. Along with exercising on your own, you will walk with your group for 15–20 min once every week.

At the end of the program, we fully expect that you will be a nonsmoker. Practice makes perfect, so you should always refer back to the techniques and strategies for managing high-risk situations and urges to smoke that you learned in group. Over time, your cravings will disappear and you will be well on your way to a longer, healthier life. We wish you the best of luck!

Chapter 2 Getting Started

Before your first group meeting, we ask that you complete a number of forms and self-assessment measures. These forms will help both you and your group leader understand the factors that maintain your smoking habits and how best to deal with them. The information garnered from these self-assessments will help in determining the best quit plan for you.

Complete and score each form in this chapter and be sure to bring them all to your first group meeting.

Medical Risk Factors

Because the last half of the program incorporates an element of weight control, we ask participants to engage in 30 min per day of moderate-intensity physical activity on most days of the week (e.g., walking at a fast pace). This amount of activity is safe for most Americans. It is the level recommended by the Centers for Disease Control (CDC) and the American Heart Association (AHA). To be on the safe side, however, we ask that you complete the Physical Activity Readiness Questionnaire (PAR-Q) (provided here). The PAR-Q is a scale that measures medical risk factors. (PAR-Q Validation Report. British Columbia Ministry of Health, May 1978.) If you answer "Yes" to one or more of the seven questions, you should obtain your medical care provider's approval before joining the group.

PAR-Q

If you are between the ages of 15 and 69, the PAR-Q will tell you whether you should check with your doctor before engaging in physical activity. Common sense is your best guide when you answer these questions. Please read them carefully and answer each one honestly by checking "Yes" or "No."

Yes	No	
_____	_____	1. Has your doctor ever said that you have a heart condition and that you should only do physical activity recommended by a doctor?
_____	_____	2. Do you feel pain in your chest when you do physical activity?
_____	_____	3. In the past month, have you had chest pain when you were not doing physical activity?
_____	_____	4. Do you lose your balance because of dizziness or do you ever lose consciousness?
_____	_____	5. Do you have a bone or joint problem (e.g., back, knee, or hip) that could be made worse by a change in your physical activity?
_____	_____	6. Is your doctor currently prescribing drugs (e.g., water pills) for high blood pressure or heart condition?
_____	_____	7. Do you know of any other reason why you should not engage in physical activity?

Your Height and Current Weight

It is important to accurately record your height and weight before beginning treatment. This will be helpful during the second phase of the program, when the meal-replacement program is introduced. You and your group leader will use your vital statistics to determine your ideal calorie intake. This will help you structure your diet and choose appropriate foods.

If possible, we recommend that you use a medical-grade scale for determining your current weight. Your group leader may have the necessary equipment and may weigh and measure you at the first meeting as well.

My Height _____

My Weight _____

Fagerstrom Test for Nicotine Dependence

This scale is a scientific measure of just how addicted to nicotine you really are.

Write the number of the answer that is most applicable on the line to the left of the question.

_____ 1. How soon after you awake do you smoke your first cigarette?

After 30 min	0
Within 30 min	1

_____ 2. Do you find it difficult to refrain from smoking in places where it is forbidden, such as the library, theater, or doctor's office?

No	0
Yes	1

_____ 3. Which of all the cigarettes you smoke in a day is the most satisfying?

Any other than the first one in the morning	0
The first one in the morning	1

_____ 4. How many cigarettes do you smoke a day?

1–15	0
16–25	1
More than 26	2

_____ 5. Do you smoke more during the morning than during the rest of the day?

No	0
Yes	1

_____ 6. Do you smoke when you are so ill that you are in bed most of the day?

No	0
Yes	1

_____ 7. Does the brand you smoke have a low, medium, or high nicotine content?

Low	0
Medium	1
High	2

_____ 8. How often do you inhale the smoke from your cigarette?

Never	0
Sometimes	1
Always	2

Scoring Instructions:

Add up your responses to all the items. Total scores should range from 0 to 11, where 7 or greater suggests physical dependence on nicotine.

TOTAL SCORE: _____

(Heatherton, T. F., Kozlowski, L. T., Frecker, R. C., Fagerstrom, K. O. (1991). The Fagerstrom test for nicotine dependence: A revision of the Fagerstrom Tolerance Questionnaire. *British Journal of Addictions, 86,* 1119–1127.)

Smoking Questionnaire

The Why Do You Smoke? questionnaire helps to assess how important various psychological reasons for smoking are for you. It can help in planning your program for quitting.

WHY DO YOU SMOKE?

Here are some statements made by people to describe what they get out of smoking cigarettes. How often do you feel this way when smoking them? Circle one number for each statement.

Important: Answer every question.

	ALWAYS	FREQUENTLY	OCCASIONALLY	SELDOM	NEVER
1. I smoke cigarettes in order to keep myself from slowing down.	5	4	3	2	1
2. Handling a cigarette is part of the enjoyment of smoking.	5	4	3	2	1
3. Smoking cigarettes is pleasant and relaxing.	5	4	3	2	1
4. I continue to smoke so that I don't gain weight.	5	4	3	2	1
5. I light up a cigarette when I feel angry about something.	5	4	3	2	1
6. When I have run out of cigarettes, I find it almost unbearable until I can get them.	5	4	3	2	1
7. I smoke cigarettes automatically without even being aware of it.	5	4	3	2	1
8. I started to smoke to control my weight.	5	4	3	2	1
9. I smoke cigarettes to stimulate me, to perk me up.	5	4	3	2	1
10. Part of the enjoyment of smoking a cigarette comes from the steps I take to light up.	5	4	3	2	1
11. If I stop smoking, I will gain weight.	5	4	3	2	1
12. I find cigarettes pleasurable.	5	4	3	2	1
13. When I feel uncomfortable or upset about something, I light up a cigarette.	5	4	3	2	1
14. I am very much aware of the fact when I am not smoking a cigarette.	5	4	3	2	1

15. I often smoke to kill my appetite when I get hungry.	5	4	3	2	1
16. I light up a cigarette without realizing I still have one burning in the ashtray.	5	4	3	2	1
17. I smoke cigarettes to give me a "lift."	5	4	3	2	1
18. When I smoke a cigarette, part of the enjoyment is watching the smoke as I exhale it.	5	4	3	2	1
19. I smoke at the end of a meal so I won't eat too much.	5	4	3	2	1
20. I want a cigarette most when I am comfortable and relaxed.	5	4	3	2	1
21. When I feel "blue" or want to take my mind off cares and worries, I smoke cigarettes.	5	4	3	2	1
22. I get a real gnawing hunger for a cigarette when I haven't smoked for a while.	5	4	3	2	1
23. I smoke instead of snacking when I am bored.	5	4	3	2	1
24. I've found a cigarette in my mouth and didn't remember putting it there.	5	4	3	2	1

HOW TO SCORE:

1. Enter the numbers you have circled to the questions in the spaces below, putting the number you have circled to Questions 1 over line 1, to Question 2 over line 2, etc.

2. Total the 3 scores on each lline to get your totals. For example, the sum of your scores over lines 1, 9, and 17 gives you your score on Stimulation - lines 2, 10, and 18 give the score on Handling, etc.

Totals

	+		+		=	
1		9		17		Stimulation
	+		+		=	
2		10		18		Handling
	+		+		=	
3		12		20		Pleasurable Relaxation
	+		+		=	
5		13		21		Crutch: Tension Reduction
	+		+		=	
6		14		22		Craving: Psychological Addiction
	+		+		=	
7		16		24		Habit

	+		+		+		+		+		=	
4		8		11		15		19		23		Weight Concern

Scores can vary from 3 to 15. Any score 11 and above is high; any score 7 and below is low.

Horn, D. H. (1969) National Clearinghouse for Smoking and Health, DHEW Publication No. (NIH) #78–1822

Reasons for Quitting

In the space provided, list your reasons for wanting to quit smoking.

1. _____
2. _____
3. _____
4. _____
5. _____
6. _____
7. _____
8. _____
9. _____
10. _____

Hughes–Hatsukami Withdrawal Questionnaire

The Hughes–Hatsukami Withdrawal Questionnaire (HHWQ) (Hughes and Hatsukami, 1986) is a valid and reliable measure of the symptoms of tobacco withdrawal. Although you have not yet quit smoking, we ask that you complete this checklist in order to determine a baseline measurement of your symptoms. We will refer to this completed questionnaire later in the program.

Use a scale of 0–4 to rate each of the following eight symptoms with reference to the past 24 hr.

	No symptom at all	Severe symptom
	0-----1-----2-----3-----4	
1.	Urges to smoke	_____
2.	Irritability, frustration, or anger	_____
3.	Anxiety or nervousness	_____
4.	Difficulty concentrating	_____
5.	Restlessness or impatience	_____
6.	Hunger	_____
7.	Insomnia or disturbed sleep	_____
8.	Depression or feeling blue	_____

Hughes, J. R., & Hatsukami, D. Signs and symptoms of tobacco withdrawal. *Archives of General Psychiatry*, 1986, 43; 289–294

Chapter 3

Session 1

Goals

- To learn about this program and what it will involve

- To gain insight into your reasons for smoking and wanting to quit

- To learn to self-monitor your smoking habits using Pack-Wraps

- To understand the link between smoking and weight gain

Overview

You are about to take part in a 16-week program designed to help you quit smoking without gaining weight. The first part of this program is focused on helping you to end your smoking habit. You, along with the other members of your group, will be asked to smoke your last cigarette 4 weeks from today. We strongly recommend that you do **not** try to quit smoking before then. We want you to have enough time to prepare so that when the time comes, you are absolutely ready. If you try to quit too soon, you may not be entirely successful. It is important to go slowly, give it your best shot, and build the skills and confidence you need to be successful.

In addition to helping you give up smoking, this group will also help you:

- Increase your understanding of the smoking cessation process—what to expect, what will be hard, and what will help

- Increase understanding and gradually begin to modify your smoking pattern—by understanding what triggers each cigarette and how those habit chains can be broken up

- Share ideas and problem solve

- Share information

- Provide support

- Learn new ways to handle difficult situations

In the second phase of this program, you will learn ways of managing your weight. You will use a meal replacement program designed for you specifically, based on your ideal calorie intake. The ideal calorie intake is the number of calories you need per day in order to maintain your current weight. You will also begin incorporating physical activity into your routine.

Throughout this program, you will be expected to complete at-home exercises. These exercises are important because they will help you to better understand your smoking habits. The more you can learn about what is keeping you hooked on cigarettes, the more successful you will be in your attempt to quit. A large part of this program's success depends upon your ability to complete homework assignments.

Reasons for Smoking

Physical Addiction

Nicotine is a drug that has many effects. It reduces anxiety and irritability, boosts concentration, and suppresses appetite. All smokers get at least some of these effects and some are more dependent on them than others. Physical dependence on nicotine is an addiction.

Refer back to your completed Fagerstrom Scale from the previous chapter. If your score is 7 or higher, you may be physically dependent on nicotine. In addition, the following signs suggest that a smoker is physiologically dependent on nicotine.

- Smoking within less than 1 hour after awakening

- Smoking heavily

- Inhaling deeply

- Using high-nicotine brands of cigarettes

- Finding the first cigarette of the day the most gratifying

If you are addicted to nicotine, quitting smoking is going to be difficult. It is going to be hard work, but the benefits are well worth the effort. Be prepared for withdrawal symptoms right after quitting. Remember that these symptoms will be more intense during the first week of cessation. You can expect symptoms to mostly dissipate after 1 week and entirely dissipate after approximately 1 month.

Psychological Dependence

As just discussed, some smokers are physically dependent on nicotine. However, all smokers are psychologically dependent on cigarettes. Smoking is a habit that is threaded through a person's entire lifestyle. Smoking can become so automatic that many smokers forget that each cigarette involves a choice. You can choose not to smoke. You can choose to do something else.

Why Do You Smoke?

Turn to your completed smoking questionnaire from the previous chapter. Review your answers and evaluate the motives that trigger your smoking behavior. The more you learn about what causes you to smoke, the more ready you will be to break the habit.

Reasons for Quitting Smoking

Refer back to the list of reasons for quitting smoking that you created before beginning treatment (see previous chapter). What sorts of reasons did you list?

Health Consequences

The number-one reason most people give for wanting to quit is to improve health. Smoking is a dangerous habit. More than 60,000 studies link smoking to heart disease, cancer, and lung disease. If you quit now, you can undo much of the damage. If you quit smoking today and do not develop smoking-related illness within 5 years, you may live as long as someone who has never smoked.

Setting a Good Example

Some people quit smoking to set a good example for their loved ones who smoke or are at risk for taking up smoking. If you have children, you should know that kids with parents who smoke are more likely than others to pick up the habit and less likely to quit.

Aesthetics

Let's face it, smoking is unattractive. It makes your clothes and hair smell, yellows your teeth and fingers, and gives you bad breath. If you quit smoking, you will reap the benefits of an improved physical appearance, a cleaner and fresher-smelling home, and whiter teeth, in addition to the most important benefit of all—a longer, healthier life.

Sense of Accomplishment

Smokers who quit successfully feel proud and good about themselves. It is helpful to view smoking as a challenge to be mastered. Conquering smoking shows that you can exercise control over your life.

Social Acceptance

Quitting smoking will earn you approval from other nonsmokers and reduce inconvenience. With the enactment of strict, no-smoking laws in various states, it is almost impossible for smokers to practice their habit in restaurants and bars, among other establishments. If you quit smoking, you will no longer have to run outside for "cigarette breaks."

Finances

Think of how much you will save by not needing to buy cigarettes! Plus, many health and life insurance companies charge lower premiums to nonsmokers.

Safety

Quitting smoking also helps reduce the risk of home and office fires, auto accidents (a lot of people smoke while driving and this can be distracting), and burns that damage clothing or cause injury.

Pack-Wraps

Monitoring your smoking habit is the first step in quitting successfully. Starting today, you will use Pack-Wraps to track your smoking. These cards are designed with enough space to record each cigarette you smoke during the day. Insert a Pack-Wrap into your pack or use a rubber band to wrap it around the outside. Each time you smoke, **before** you actually light up, make a note on the Pack-Wrap. Be sure to record the time of day you smoked, as well as the circumstances (situational and emotional) in which you smoked. Also rate how much you felt you "needed" each cigarette on a scale of 1 to 3 with 1 being "very strongly needed" and 3 being "weakly needed."

The information you write down will help you and your group leader better understand your smoking pattern. It will show how soon in the morning you smoke, how long you go between cigarettes and whether this varies across the day, and where you are most likely to smoke (while driving, with a cup of coffee, after a meal, etc.). This information will be important when designing your quit plan.

We have included a blank Pack-Wrap at the end of the chapter for your use. You may tear it or cut it out of the book. Because you will complete a new one every day, we have provided additional copies in the appendix at the end of the book. If you need more, you may make photocopies.

Quitting Smoking Without Gaining Weight

Although the most important goal of this program is quitting smoking, we do recognize that most women would like to retain a graceful figure and not gain any weight after quitting. The average weight gain after quitting smoking is about 8 lbs, but some people do gain more. Two factors cause the ex-smoker to gain weight: (1) eating more; and (2) a decrease in the body's ability to burn calories (slowed metabolism).

Once you have become a secure nonsmoker, you will be introduced to a new part of the program that deals with weight gain. During the second part of the program, you will start a meal replacement plan that will prevent you from eating more. We will also introduce an exercise program that will prevent your metabolism from slowing down. You will learn more about this phase of the program as the time for it gets closer. You will be introduced to the meal replacement program in approximately 7 weeks.

Homework

✎ Complete Pack-Wraps on a daily basis over the course of the week and bring them to the next meeting.

✎ Complete the Self-Efficacy Questionnaire.

Self-Efficacy Questionnaire

Instructions: Please rate each of the following items on the scale on the right to indicate how sure you are that you would be able to resist smoking in that situation. Circle the appropriate response.

Item	Completely Unsure						Completely Sure
1. When you feel impatient	1	2	3	4	5	6	7
2. When you are waiting for someone or something	1	2	3	4	5	6	7
3. When you feel frustrated	1	2	3	4	5	6	7
4. When you are worried	1	2	3	4	5	6	7
5. When you want something in your mouth	1	2	3	4	5	6	7
6. When you want to cheer up	1	2	3	4	5	6	7
7. When you want to keep yourself busy	1	2	3	4	5	6	7
8. When you are trying to pass time	1	2	3	4	5	6	7
9. When someone offers you a cigarette	1	2	3	4	5	6	7
10. When you are drinking an alcoholic beverage	1	2	3	4	5	6	7
11. When you feel uncomfortable	1	2	3	4	5	6	7
12. When you feel embarrassed	1	2	3	4	5	6	7
13. When you are in a situation in which you feel smoking is a part of your self-image	1	2	3	4	5	6	7
14. When you want to feel more mature and sophisticated	1	2	3	4	5	6	7

Yates, A. J & Thain J. (1985) Self-efficacy as a predictor of relapse following voluntary cessation of smoking. Addictive Behaviors. 10(3), 291–298

Assignment: Pack-Wraps

Wrap this daily cigarette count sheet around your pack of cigarettes and secure it with a rubber band. When you are about to take a cigarette, before you actually put it in your mouth and light up, indicate the following:

1)   **Time of day**
2)   **Activity you are involved in**
3)   **Word/words that best describe your feeling at the time**
4)   **How much do you need that particular cigarette:**

1 – **Very Strongly needed**   2 – **Strongly Needed**   3 – **Weakly Needed**

# of Cigarette	Time	Food/Alcohol	Relaxation	Work	Social	Driving	Other (please describe)	Angry	Anxious	Bored	Depressed	Frustrated	Happy	Relaxed	Tired	Need Rating		
1																1	2	3
2																1	2	3
3																1	2	3
4																1	2	3
5																1	2	3
6																1	2	3
7																1	2	3
8																1	2	3
9																1	2	3
10																1	2	3
11																1	2	3
12																1	2	3
13																1	2	3
14																1	2	3
15																1	2	3
16																1	2	3
17																1	2	3
18																1	2	3
19																1	2	3
20																1	2	3

Chapter 4   *Session 2*

Goals

- To review your completed Pack-Wraps in order to better understand your unique smoking habit

- To determine your least and most desired cigarettes of the day and the triggers for your smoking

- To design a plan for gradually reducing the number of cigarettes you smoke

- To begin the quit process

Pack-Wrap Review

Today you will review your completed Pack-Wraps during the group meeting. Look for any patterns in your smoking. Your Pack-Wraps should reveal categories of activities, situations, thoughts, or feelings that trigger your smoking. You may find that you have more than one kind of trigger.

Here is a list of common triggers for smoking. Review this list and see whether any of these apply to you. Discuss your triggers with the group.

- talking on the telephone

- getting up in the morning

- drinking coffee

- waiting for a bus or train

- the end of a meal

- drinking an alcoholic beverage

- experiencing a difficult situation (at home or work)

- as a break in the day

- being under time pressure

- in social situations with friends

- feeling angry, frustrated, or anxious

- feeling sad

- boredom

- leaving work

- watching TV

- after sex

- gaining weight

- driving

Once you have identified your triggers and discussed them with the group, review your completed Pack-Wraps again, but this time identify the cigarettes you rated as most desired or needed and those you rated as least desired or needed. Later in the session, you will work with your group leader to choose certain cigarettes to eliminate or modify. If your most desired cigarette is one you smoke first thing in the morning, this suggests that you are physically addicted to nicotine. It probably will be very hard for you to give this particular cigarette up, so your group leader will work with you to identify others that you can eliminate more easily.

Self-Efficacy

Self-efficacy describes a person's confidence that she can produce a desired outcome. In the case of smoking cessation, self-efficacy indicates confidence about being able to quit smoking. Your belief in your ability to quit smoking positively influences your likelihood of success.

Your homework assignment for the last session was to complete the Self-Efficacy Questionnaire in the previous chapter. This questionnaire asked you to rate how confident you are about being able to resist smoking in each of 14 situations. Review your answers and note your overall level of self-efficacy about quitting. Also take note of your individual responses regarding your ability to resist the temptation to smoke in certain situations. Discuss with the other members of your group the situations in which you are most worried about being able to smoke.

Ways to Quit

Tapering

In this session, you and the members of the group will take the first step in designing a quit plan. Your group leader will recommend that you start off by gradually reducing the number of cigarettes you smoke every day until the quit date. This is called a tapering plan. For example, if you currently smoke 15 cigarettes a day, a tapering plan might eliminate 1 cigarette every day for 1 week. In part, tapering lets you gradually become used to having less nicotine in your body. It also gives you the opportunity to practice smoking less and builds your confidence about being able to change your smoking behavior.

Which cigarettes should be eliminated first? This decision can be made in a number of ways.

Need Ratings—Refer back to your completed Pack-Wraps. What cigarettes did you rate the *lowest* in terms of level of desire or need? One good way to start the tapering plan is to first eliminate low- or modest-need cigarettes.

Trigger Categories—Alternatively, you can rank order your smoking trigger categories from 1 through 5, in order of how challenging they will be to resist. Then, pick one of the least challenging trigger categories and start to experiment with something we call "stimulus control." What this means is choosing some situations that normally serve as triggers and making them incompatible with smoking. For example, you can declare certain rooms or zones of your house as "no-smoking zones." If you smoke while driving, you can gradually turn your car into a no-smoking zone by setting limits such as not allowing yourself to light up before you reach a certain landmark. Every time you drive, you can gradually increase the distance of the landmark from your home or office. Or, you can substitute other activities in place of smoking. You can chew gum or have a piece of candy instead.

Time Between Cigarettes—Some people find that their easiest way to cut down on smoking is to set a time limit between cigarettes. Use the Pack-Wraps to decide what time limit is reasonable. Or set a "good night" time after which no cigarettes will be smoked. You can always just go to bed if you have the urge to smoke.

Cold Turkey

We understand that some people may find tapering a bit frustrating, but we strongly encourage you to give it a try rather than attempting to quit "cold turkey." As the saying goes, "Practice makes perfect." If you find it difficult to cut down on cigarettes, you can start off by resisting smoking in some situations in which you normally do smoke (e.g., while on the phone or with a cup of coffee) Even if you don't eliminate any cigarettes before the quit date in 3 weeks, if you can stop yourself from smoking in some trigger situations, you will be better prepared to make the change to total cessation.

What to Change This Week

In the upcoming week, we want you to begin your tapering plan. To review, you will be eliminating your least desired or needed cigarettes. In addition, we would like you to try resisting the urge to smoke some of the cigarettes you feel you need or want the most (those rated a level 3). Try to postpone smoking a few of these cigarettes for 5–10 min after you first experience an urge or craving. Over the course of the week, you can gradually increase this delay.

It's also a good idea to taper down your caffeine intake. The reason for this is that caffeine and nicotine work in similar ways. This can cause two different problems later on. First, as you cut down and quit smoking, your ability to tolerate caffeine will decrease. This means that the amount of coffee, tea, or cola you once tolerated with ease can now trigger symptoms of anxiety and shakiness. In other words, caffeine can throw you into what feel like symptoms of nicotine withdrawal. Second, having caffeine in the body can trigger cravings for nicotine. For these reasons, it's a good idea to use the next 3 weeks to cut back on your caffeine intake.

It's important that you don't try to eliminate caffeine from your diet in one fell swoop. Since caffeine is also a moderately powerful drug, discontinuing it too fast will cause symptoms like headaches, fatigue, and depression. Instead, try substituting decaffeinated beverages for some of the day's coffee, tea, or soda. You can gradually increase the ratio of decaffeinated to caffeinated drinks you consume.

Homework

✎ Continue filling out Pack-Wraps on a daily basis over the course of the week and bring them to the next meeting.

✎ Begin your tapering plan.

Chapter 5

Session 3

Goals

- To review your completed Pack-Wraps and discuss your experience with the tapering plan

- To learn strategies that will help you avoid smoking

- To practice diaphragmatic breathing as a way to reduce anxiety during withdrawal

Pack-Wrap Review

Today you will review your completed Pack-Wraps to see if you were able to gradually decrease your daily number of cigarettes over the course of the last week. We know that following the tapering plan may have been difficult and that you may have encountered situations in which it was hard for you to resist smoking. This is normal and to be expected. It is also normal to be experiencing withdrawal symptoms if you were successful in cutting back on your smoking last week. If you are feeling anxious or irritable or are having trouble concentrating, this is just a sign that you are making progress toward your goal of quitting smoking. Your withdrawal symptoms will steadily decrease over time as you approach the group quit date.

Diaphragmatic Breathing

Many physical symptoms of anxiety can be reduced by modifying breathing patterns. Stress stimulates the sympathetic nervous system—shown by rapid heart rate, sweating, muscle tension, and rapid, shallow breathing. Few of us can voluntarily slow our heart rate. But we can learn to reverse sympathetic activation by doing diaphragmatic (abdominal) breathing. Rapid, shallow "chest breathing" lowers oxygen flow and reduces transfer of nutrients to the tissues. On the other hand, deep, diaphragmatic breathing expands lung capacity, improves blood flow, and triggers a relaxation response. Your group leader will teach you a simple diaphragmatic breathing exercise that you can use to manage your anxiety throughout the withdrawal phase.

While sitting comfortably, place one hand on your chest and the other on your abdomen. Take a deep breath, making sure that the hand on your abdomen rises higher than the one on your chest. Exhale through your mouth and then take in another slow, deep breath and hold it for a count of seven. Then slowly exhale through your mouth for a count of eight. Exhaling should last twice as long as inhaling. As the last air is released, contract your abdominal muscles to dispel all the remaining air in your lungs. Try to breathe at a rate of one breath every 10 seconds. Repeat the cycle five times, twice a day.

Strategies to Avoid Smoking

In today's meeting, your group leader will talk to you about various things you can do (or not do) to avoid smoking. There are a number of strategies you can use. We encourage you to try them all and figure out which ones work best for you. Remember, this program is about gradual change. Give yourself some time to practice before you tackle the most difficult challenges.

Avoid Situations That Automatically Trigger Smoking

For the first few weeks after quitting, it is best to avoid settings like bars, parties, or casinos, where you may be surrounded by smokers. Do not sit near smokers at sports events or stand near groups of people who are smoking, like colleagues who are gathering for a cigarette break. The smell and sight of smoke, as well as peer pressure, may trigger urges to smoke. Early on in the quit process, we ask you to try to spend as much time as possible with nonsmokers and avoid friends of yours who smoke. You will not need to give up those friends entirely, nor will you need to avoid them forever. Think of a person who is just learning to ski. You wouldn't advise a brand-new skier to go down the most advanced slope on her first day on skis, would you? Being a brand-new nonsmoker around smokers is like trying to ski the most dangerous slope.

Make Cigarettes Inaccessible

If you live with a smoker, ask him or her to keep cigarettes and other smoking materials out of sight. You can also designate your car and certain areas of your home as "smoke-free." Don't smoke in your bedroom, where the smell can get into your clothes and linens. Avoid lighting up in the kitchen around food and cooking utensils. Remove the ashtray and the lighter from your car to make smoking while you are driving less convenient. You can keep your cigarettes with you while driving, but lock them in the trunk of the car. That makes it difficult to smoke because you would need to pull over and open the trunk in order to get at your cigarettes.

Take Steps to Change Your Routine

Modifying your daily routine can lessen the urge to smoke. If you usually smoke at the breakfast table while reading the paper, try reading the paper in a different location such as the living room or even outside in the fresh air if the weather is nice. If you smoke while watching television from a certain living room chair, sit in a different chair or go for a walk instead. If you smoke while talking on your home telephone, make your calls from someplace else. If your habit is to smoke right after eating a meal, get up and wash the dishes instead.

Make a Bet

Make a friendly bet with someone who can motivate you to quit. Bets do not have to be monetary. You can bet a night out (dinner and a movie), a favor (baby-sit your best friend's children while she's out with her husband), or a chore (do the dishes for a month). Think of something fun and creative that will keep you motivated to quit smoking.

Find a Buddy

Having reliable social support is a good predictor of successful quitting. You will benefit greatly from having a person whom you can call whenever the urge to smoke is strong. Another group member can be a great "buddy," as can a friend or family member who cares about your well-being.

As mentioned at the beginning of the chapter, you and others in your group may have experienced difficulty with the tapering plan. If you have concerns about your readiness to quit, discuss the concerns with the group. Others are very likely feeling the same way as you.

Quitting is a process that has only just begun. You will undoubtedly face difficulties and challenges, but you have made positive changes as well. It is helpful to recall these successes, no matter how large or small, particularly during times of doubt. That is why it is so important that you continue with your tapering plan over the course of the next week. Any cigarettes you dispense with now will make things easier next week as there will be fewer changes to make (i.e., fewer cigarettes to eliminate).

Homework

✎ Continue filling out Pack-Wraps on a daily basis over the course of the week and bring them to the next meeting.

✎ Continue your tapering plan.

✎ Practice diaphragmatic breathing twice a day to relieve anxiety related to withdrawal symptoms.

Chapter 6   *Session 4*

Goals

- To review your completed Pack-Wraps and discuss your latest experience with the tapering plan

- To learn additional strategies that will help you avoid smoking

- To prepare to quit smoking next week

Pack-Wrap Review

As you have done at the start of the last few sessions, you will once again review your completed Pack-Wraps to see whether you were able to further reduce the number of cigarettes you smoke daily. Any challenges you previously faced should have become less difficult. If you had difficulty cutting back on your smoking, that is okay. Sometimes, the early stages of the quitting process can feel like you are riding a rollercoaster. You may experience many ups and downs, but eventually you will hit a plateau.

If you are suffering from physical symptoms of withdrawal, be sure to practice the diaphragmatic breathing exercise you learned last week (see Chapter 5). This exercise will combat your anxiety and help you relax.

Additional Strategies to Avoid Smoking

In today's meeting, your group leader will show you additional ways of avoiding smoking. You should use these in conjunction with the strategies you learned last week.

Alternatives to Smoking

When the urge to smoke arises, it will pass faster and easier if you immediately do something else. Some examples of alternative things to do are:

- take deep breaths—this is relaxing and will often make the craving go away

- chew on a straw

- drink water

- chew on ice chips

- chew on a cinnamon stick

- eat a sugarless piece of candy

- chew sugarless gum

- engage in physical activity—go for a walk

- telephone a friend

- pick up a hobby—doing something like drawing, sewing, or knitting will keep your hands busy

Mentally Talk Yourself Through the Urge

If you have the urge to smoke, it is helpful to remind yourself of the positive aspects or advantages to quitting smoking. Follow these steps any time you feel the urge to smoke.

1. Mentally review your reasons for wanting to quit (refer back to the list you created in Chapter 2).

2. Make the task manageable. Think of it as forgetting about the craving for 5 min at a time, giving up just this one cigarette, or quitting for just 1 day at a time.

3. Coach yourself through a craving by saying:

   "I can meet this challenge."

   "I can handle this one."

   "This feeling is a signal that I am doing something good for myself."

4. Make reinforcing self-statements. Pat yourself on the back!

   "I did it! I managed not to have a cigarette."

   "It wasn't as bad as I expected."

   "I've gotten through another day."

Pamper Yourself Now

Giving up smoking is difficult. It is crucial that you find ways to reward yourself throughout the quitting process. Use the space provided to write down some ideas for rewards. Some examples of rewards are: treating yourself to a movie, concert, or play, luxuriating in a bubble bath, sleeping late, buying flowers for your home or office, getting a manicure and pedicure, etc.

My Rewards

1. _____
2. _____
3. _____
4. _____
5. _____
6. _____
7. _____
8. _____
9. _____
10. _____

Plan for a Special Reward

In addition to giving yourself small rewards, why not come up with a special luxury that you have always wanted? Plan to reward yourself with it once you have been a nonsmoker for several months. Maybe you have dreamed about taking a trip to Hawaii, or maybe you have your eye on a new bedroom set. Calculate how much money you will save by not smoking and put this amount toward your special reward.

What to Expect Next Week

Next week is the quit date. You and the other members of your group will smoke your last cigarette at the beginning of the next session. You will do this to make a clean break and to demonstrate in a kind of ceremony that you are making a pact with each other to say good-bye to smoking. If you wish to start your day smoke-free, rather than quit at the next group meeting, you may smoke your final cigarette the evening before. You are encouraged to attend the group quit "ceremony" regardless so you can share the experience and support the other members.

Homework

✎ Continue filling out Pack-Wraps on a daily basis over the course of the week and bring them to the next meeting.

✎ Continue your tapering plan.

✎ Practice diaphragmatic breathing twice a day to relieve anxiety related to withdrawal symptoms.

Chapter 7

Session 5

Goals

- To smoke your last cigarette!

- To learn how to manage symptoms of nicotine withdrawal

- To review your reasons for wanting to quit smoking

- To learn to cope with last-minute fears and doubts about quitting

Smoking Your Last Cigarette

The time has finally come! Today is your quit date. At the start of today's session, you and the other members of your group will assemble outside to smoke your last cigarette.

If you decided to quit last night, you may find it difficult to join your group members as they smoke. The choice is up to you. You are encouraged to participate in the "ceremony," however, as it can be helpful to experience the camaraderie of being part of the group event.

Nicotine Withdrawal Symptoms

The focus of this week's meeting is the symptoms of nicotine withdrawal and ways to manage them. It is important to note that not everyone experiences withdrawal symptoms. Also, symptoms can vary widely in terms of when they occur, how intense they are, and how long they last. Some people may have an easy time, whereas others may have a more difficult time.

The first week after quitting is the most difficult. It is important to understand that you will probably feel worse in the earlier part of the week than you will in the later part. Some of the more common symptoms that you may experience in the forthcoming week are described in the sections that follow.

Nervousness or Tension

Anxiety and nervousness are symptoms of how the body responds to the withdrawal of nicotine. Also, those symptoms are often made worse by worries about quitting. To reduce nervousness and tension that are brought about by nicotine withdrawal, you should increase your physical activity and use the diaphragmatic breathing exercise you learned 2 weeks ago (see Chapter 5). It is also recommended that you gradually reduce (or avoid) caffeine, which can make anxiety worse, especially during the withdrawal process.

Irritability

Anger, shortened temper, and irritability occur frequently as nicotine withdrawal symptoms. Those symptoms can be especially problematic when they cause people to act in ways that strain their personal and professional relationships. To manage irritability, you can take walks, use diaphragmatic breathing exercises, and also give yourself permission to take a "time-out" when distressed. You may find it helpful to ask your family and friends to anticipate your crankiness and to be a little tolerant during the quit-smoking process.

Lethargy or Tiredness

The first week of quitting might be accompanied by feelings of tiredness and lethargy. Getting extra sleep, increasing activity level, and trying, as much as possible, to avoid highly stressful situations are all techniques that you can use to manage feelings of low energy.

Increased Hunger or Food Cravings

Many people experience increased hunger and food cravings during the process of quitting smoking. Increased desire for sweet, high-carbohydrate snacks is especially common, although other kinds of foods can be craved and overeaten as well. There may be several reasons for increased hunger, including chemical changes in the brain that result from the decrease in nicotine in the body. Some people may use eating as a substitute for smoking, while others may use food as a reward for not smoking. Regardless of the reason, you should expect that you will experience increased hunger and food cravings during the quit-smoking process.

Later on in the program, you will begin using a meal replacement program to help maintain your weight. In the meantime, you can manage your hunger sensibly by eating three regular meals a day and incorporating healthy, low-calorie snacks such as popcorn or pretzels into your diet. Drink lots of water or diet beverages to curb your hunger and deter your cravings. Try also to engage in pleasurable activities besides eating, such as working on a hobby or going for walks.

Lack of Concentration

After quitting smoking, some people experience problems concentrating. Concentration troubles arise partly from direct effects of nicotine withdrawal on the central nervous system. To reduce concentration problems, you should avoid consuming alcohol. You may also try deep breathing and exercising to increase oxygen flow to the brain.

Cigarette Craving

Cravings to smoke can be one of the more troublesome and long-lasting symptoms associated with quitting smoking. Often, cravings are triggered by cues that you have learned to associate with smoking. It is important to remember that although the urge to smoke can feel overwhelming, it passes quickly. To stop the craving and prevent it from transforming into action, some people find it helpful to snap a rubber band and mentally say "Stop!" The best defense is to switch attention to something else, preferably something pleasant, and, if possible, to move away from any cues that have habitually triggered smoking.

Some less common symptoms of nicotine withdrawal that you may experience are outlined in the following sections.

Trouble Sleeping

Some people have difficulty either falling asleep or staying asleep. Good ways to manage sleep difficulties are to increase physical activity during the day, reduce caffeine intake, take a hot bath before bedtime, or use deep breathing exercises to fall asleep.

Cough

Some people complain or become frightened by increased coughing during the early stages of quitting. Increased coughing is a sign that the lungs are cleaning themselves of tar. If you experience coughing, you can use cough drops or sugar-free hard candy.

Sore Throat

Some people experience a dry, sore throat. Increasing liquid intake and using cough drops are helpful.

Constipation

Constipation during the first 10 days of the withdrawal process can be troublesome to some people. Nicotine acts as a laxative. Without it, you may experience constipation until your body adapts. Increased water and fiber intake, continued exercise, and a mild over-the-counter laxative can be helpful in managing constipation.

Headache

If you find that you are experiencing headaches, try to get extra rest and use your deep breathing exercises. Aspirin can also be helpful.

How to Get Through the Next Week

There is no denying that the next week is going to be difficult. That's why it is so important for you to outline a detailed plan for avoiding smoking over the course of the next several days. What specific things will you do to keep yourself from lighting up?

Think about any high-risk situations you may face in the forthcoming week. Are you attending any parties where alcohol may be served and people may be smoking? Do you have a work deadline that may cause you stress? What situations are likely to present the greatest difficulty for you?

Not smoking is a skill that you will become more expert at with practice. Now is the time to try out lots of different strategies to see what works. Your group leader will review your plan and make suggestions.

Tracking Your Withdrawal Symptoms

You will remember that you completed the Hughes–Hatsukami Withdrawal Questionnaire at the beginning of the program. This questionnaire measures tobacco withdrawal symptoms, like the ones previously discussed. Now that you have quit smoking, you should complete the questionnaire again to keep tabs on whether your withdrawal symptoms are worsening. Later, as your body gets used to being without nicotine, you will use the checklist to track how the symptoms go away. A copy of the questionnaire is provided at the end of the chapter.

Coping with Last-Minute Fears and Doubts About Quitting

Your first smoke-free week, especially the first 48 hours, will be the most difficult. Keep reminding yourself that whatever time you endure as a nonsmoker is an investment in getting through the worst. Holding on as a nonsmoker makes it possible for things to become easier. Having one cigarette just restarts the clock and makes it necessary to endure the worst of nicotine withdrawal all over again.

You may wish to exchange contact information with the other members of your group so you can call each other when things get rough.

Homework

 ✎ Continue filling out Pack-Wraps on a daily basis over the course of the week and bring them to the next meeting.

✎ Complete the Hughes–Hatsukami Withdrawal Questionnaire to assess your withdrawal symptoms.

Hughes–Hatsukami Withdrawal Questionnaire

Use a scale of 0–4 to rate each of the following eight symptoms with reference to the past 24 hr.

No symptom at all	Severe symptom
0-----1-----2-----3-----4	

1. Urges to smoke _____

2. Irritability, frustration, or anger _____

3. Anxiety or nervousness _____

4. Difficulty concentrating _____

5. Restlessness or impatience _____

6. Hunger _____

7. Insomnia or disturbed sleep _____

8. Depression or feeling blue _____

Chapter 8

Session 6

Goals

- To review your first week without cigarettes
- To take note of your withdrawal symptoms and how you are managing them
- To begin relapse prevention planning
- To prepare to start the meal replacement program in 2 weeks

The First Week of Abstinence

How was your first week of being a nonsmoker? Were you successful in maintaining abstinence for 7 days? If so, congratulations are in order. You have reached a significant milestone in the quit-smoking process. Remember, risk of relapse is greatest in the earliest days of quitting.

If you experienced some slips in the last week, that's okay. As long as you are still committed to quitting and continue to attend group meetings, you have every opportunity to be successful. As mentioned last week, quitting smoking is a skill that requires practice. If you continue to work at it, it will get easier and easier.

If you found that your slips occurred during high-risk situations, you may think about using one of the following strategies the next time you are faced with a difficult situation.

- avoiding situations that automatically trigger smoking
- mentally talking through the urge
- doing things that are incompatible with smoking

- using rewards to stay focused on abstinence

- exercising

- talking with friends

Managing Withdrawal Symptoms

Take a look at the Hughes–Hatsukami Withdrawal Questionnaire you completed as homework. Review your withdrawal symptoms and discuss them with the group. Remember, symptoms are normal and will eventually go away. If you were able to remain abstinent for all 7 days, you will notice a decline in your negative mood by the end of the week. If you are having trouble dealing with symptoms, refer back to the coping strategies presented in the previous chapter. To help alleviate symptoms of nicotine withdrawal, minimize your intake of caffeinated drinks, avoid alcohol, get enough rest, and engage in physical activity.

How to Prevent Relapse

Now that you are well on your way to becoming a nonsmoker, it is important to address issues of relapse. The topic of relapse prevention will be the focus of the next couple of sessions. Following are three ideas that can help you remain abstinent from smoking.

Lapse versus Relapse

A *lapse* or "slip" is a misstep in the quit-smoking process. A slip can be a puff of a cigarette, a cigarette or two, or even an entire pack smoked under a provocative circumstance—like a stressful situation or a party. Slips are not the same thing as a failure or a full *relapse* to smoking. However, this does not mean slips are okay. A slip signifies that you were in a situation that exceeded your level of skill at remaining a nonsmoker. A slip is a critically important signal. If you experience a slip, take time out to understand the circumstances that surrounded the event and develop alternative ways to manage similar situations, should they occur in the future. Slips are like forest fires. It is best for all parties if they don't occur. They are costly and they make life harder. But if they do occur, do your best to put them out and to learn from them, so that they don't happen again.

Quitting is no "Small Potatoes"

Quitting smoking is no "small potatoes." Many smokers smoke throughout the day while doing many different things. Consequently, quitting smoking involves a major lifestyle change. Quitting is stressful and difficult. That is why so many people experience trouble with quitting and struggle with some ambivalent feelings. For example, many individuals miss the comforts of smoking even though they recognize its hazardous effects. You may feel the same way. This is natural, but ought to be balanced by focusing on what is being gained by quitting—a longer, healthier life.

Short-Term versus Long-Term Gains

At times you may find yourself in a difficult situation and think to yourself, "If I just have one cigarette, it will help me over this hump." That thought is a trap! Although smoking a cigarette might alleviate some current withdrawal symptoms (short-term benefit), smoking actually prolongs the process of withdrawal. Lighting up and reexposing the body to nicotine restarts the clock for the worst phase of withdrawal symptoms. That just makes it more difficult to reach the long-term goal of abstinence. In addition, smoking a cigarette or two can undermine your self-confidence and weaken your resolve to quit.

Preparing for the Meal Replacement Plan

You will soon be introduced to the weight maintenance phase of the program. It is important to remember that this phase is **not** about losing weight. It is about maintaining your current weight while pursuing the most important goal of becoming a nonsmoker. If you wish to pursue weight loss after this program is over, we encourage you to talk to your group leader or primary care physician at the appropriate time. For now, your main focus needs to be on quitting smoking, with the secondary focus being to not gain weight.

For next week's meeting, you will need to compute your ideal daily calorie intake in order to determine how much food to order through the meal replacement plan. You can accomplish this by using the Mifflin-St Jeor equation on the next page. This predictive energy equation provides an estimate of basal energy expenditure (BEE), also called the basal metabolic rate (BMR). Hospitals and nutrition clinics routinely use this equation to determine the calorie requirements of various patients.

Female

$$BMR = (10 \times \text{weight in kg}) + (6.25 \times \text{height in cm})$$
$$- (5 \times \text{age in years}) - 161$$

These equations require the weight in kilograms, the height in centimeters, and the age in years. To convert pounds to kilograms, use the following formula: lbs/2.2 = kilograms, or use the conversion shown in Table 8.1. To calculate the height in centimeters, consult the conversion chart shown in Table 8.2. To determine total daily calorie needs, the BMR (the result of the equation) has to be multiplied by the appropriate activity factor, as follows:

- 1.200 = sedentary (little or no exercise)

- 1.550 = moderately active (moderate exercise or sports 3–5 days/week)

- 1.725 = very active (hard exercise or sports 6–7 days a week)

- 1.900 = extra active (very hard exercise or sports and physical job)

Once you have determined your calorie intake level, subtract 150 calories to compensate for losing nicotine's action of burning 150 calories per day. Also subtract the number of calories per day that come from drinking alcoholic beverages. The total calories remaining is the amount of meal replacement food you will order and eat per day once the meal plan begins in 2 weeks. Please note—you may round the number up or down in order to avoid fractions.

Review the following example to see the steps involved in determining the ideal calorie intake for a 30-year-old woman, who is 5′6″ tall, weighs 135 lbs, leads a moderately active lifestyle, and doesn't drink alcohol.

$$BMR = (10 \times 61.4\,\text{kg}) + (6.25 \times 167.64\,\text{cm}) - (5 \times 30) - 161$$

$$BMR = 614 + 1047.75 - 150 - 161$$

$$BMR = 1350.75$$

$$1350.75 \times 1.550 = 2093.66$$

$$2093.66 - 150 = 1943.66$$

Ideal calorie intake = 1,945 calories per day

Table 8.1 Converting Pounds to Kilograms

Pounds	Kilograms
1.00	0.45
10.00	4.54
20.00	9.07
30.00	13.61
40.00	18.14
50.00	22.68
60.00	27.22
70.00	31.75
80.00	36.29
90.00	40.82
100.00	45.36
110.00	49.90
120.00	54.43
130.00	58.97
140.00	63.50
150.00	68.04
160.00	72.57
170.00	77.11
180.00	81.65
190.00	86.18
200.00	90.72

Table 8.2 Converting Feet and Inches to Centimeters

Feet and inches	Centimeters
2 feet 0 inches	60.96
2 feet 1 inches	63.50
2 feet 2 inches	66.04
2 feet 3 inches	68.58
2 feet 4 inches	71.12
2 feet 5 inches	73.66
2 feet 6 inches	76.20
2 feet 7 inches	78.74
2 feet 8 inches	81.28
2 feet 9 inches	83.82
2 feet 10 inches	86.36
2 feet 11 inches	88.90
3 feet 0 inches	91.44
3 feet 1 inches	93.98
3 feet 2 inches	96.52

continued

Table 8.2 Converting Feet and Inches to Centimeters *continued*

Feet and inches	Centimeters
3 feet 3 inches	99.06
3 feet 4 inches	101.60
3 feet 5 inches	104.14
3 feet 6 inches	106.68
3 feet 7 inches	109.22
3 feet 8 inches	111.76
3 feet 9 inches	114.30
3 feet 10 inches	116.84
3 feet 11 inches	119.38
4 feet 0 inches	121.92
4 feet 1 inches	124.46
4 feet 2 inches	127.00
4 feet 3 inches	129.54
4 feet 4 inches	132.08
4 feet 5 inches	134.62
4 feet 6 inches	137.16
4 feet 7 inches	139.70
4 feet 8 inches	142.24
4 feet 9 inches	144.78
4 feet 10 inches	147.32
4 feet 11 inches	149.86
5 feet 0 inches	152.40
5 feet 1 inches	154.94
5 feet 2 inches	157.48
5 feet 3 inches	160.02
5 feet 4 inches	162.56
5 feet 5 inches	165.10
5 feet 6 inches	167.64
5 feet 7 inches	170.18
5 feet 8 inches	172.72
5 feet 9 inches	175.26
5 feet 10 inches	177.80
5 feet 11 inches	180.34
6 feet 0 inches	182.88

Homework

✎ Continue filling out Pack-Wraps on a daily basis over the course of the week and bring them to the next meeting.

✎ Continue completing the Hughes–Hatsukami Withdrawal Questionnaire to assess your withdrawal symptoms. A copy of the scale is provided at the end of the chapter.

✎ Measure your height and weight and compute you ideal daily calorie intake using the Mifflin-St Jeor equation. You will place your food order next week so you can begin the meal replacement program the week after.

Hughes–Hatsukami Withdrawal Questionnaire

Use a scale of 0–4 to rate each of the following eight symptoms with reference to the past 24 hr.

0-----1-----2-----3-----4

1.	Urges to smoke	_____
2.	Irritability, frustration, or anger	_____
3.	Anxiety or nervousness	_____
4.	Difficulty concentrating	_____
5.	Restlessness or impatience	_____
6.	Hunger	_____
7.	Insomnia or disturbed sleep	_____
8.	Depression or feeling blue	_____

Hughes, J. R., & Hatsukami, D. Signs and symptoms of tobacco withdrawal. *Archives of General Psychiatry,* 1986, 43; 289–294

Chapter 9   *Session 7*

Goals

- To continue relapse prevention planning

- To learn about the upcoming physical activity program and meal replacement plan

- To begin using the Daily Diary to track your habits

Relapse Prevention

It takes effort to be successful at quitting smoking. Do not underestimate the amount of effort that is required to stay abstinent. The following sections outline ways of dealing with high-risk situations and temptations to smoke.

Coping with Social Situations

Social situations, including parties, can be very challenging for a new nonsmoker because the sight and smell of other people smoking cigarettes can create a strong urge to smoke. We advise you to try to avoid parties, bars, and other smoke-filled places during the first few weeks of your quit attempt. As weeks pass, however, avoiding all those situations and all those friends who smoke becomes less realistic. When you must attend social events in which you previously smoked, it is important to generate a plan ahead of time that will help you remain abstinent.

The following recommendations can help you avoid smoking in social situations:

- Drink something non-alcoholic or limit the amount of alcohol consumed. This is important because drinking is associated with smoking and triggers cigarette cravings for many people. Also, becoming intoxicated tends to diminish self-control and, with it, the resolve to stay smoke-free.

- Tell others at the party that you are a recent nonsmoker. Many will respond positively and praise you for your accomplishment. Also, making a public declaration renders you less likely to "slip" and have a cigarette.

- Before the event, visualize yourself at the event and not smoking. Seeing yourself in your "mind's eye" is one of the best ways to plan out how to manage difficult situations. As you visualize the event, think about who is there and what you will be talking about. Most importantly, visualize yourself successfully managing the urge to smoke.

- Enlist the help of a "buddy." In difficult social situations, the support of a buddy can make the difference between resisting a cigarette and smoking it. Getting support provides a shoulder to lean on if needed and helps to create a social context incompatible with smoking.

Coping With Feelings

You may be struggling to manage feelings that were previously alleviated or enhanced by smoking. Smoking commonly moderates the following feelings:

- boredom
- frustration
- anger
- loneliness
- happiness
- fatigue
- restlessness
- feeling cooped-up

You will discuss with the group the feelings you have been experiencing and how you have been managing them without smoking.

The Physical Activity Program

Today, your group leader will introduce you to the physical activity program and address four questions: Why? What type of activity? How much or how fast? When?

Why?

1. Participating in physical activities can reduce symptoms of nicotine withdrawal and help you cope with cravings.

2. Physical activity can become an alternative healthy reward in place of smoking or eating.

3. Physical activity helps prevent weight gain by preventing metabolism from slowing down when nicotine is withdrawn from the body.

What Type of Physical Activity?

Guidelines for health and fitness prepared by the Centers for Disease Control (CDC) and the American College of Sports Medicine (ACSM) say that every American should engage in 30 min of moderate-intensity activity on at least 5 days of the week, preferably every day. However, you don't need to start by being active for 30 min all at once. You can build up to that goal by accumulating short bouts of activity throughout the day. The goal is for the bouts to total 30 min by the end of the day. Following is a list of possible activities that can help you meet the activity goal. Experiment with a variety of activities so you can determine which ones fit your interests and lifestyle. At the beginning of next week, your group will begin a walking program together as a fun way to get everybody moving.

Light-Intensity Activities:

- Walking slowly
- Golf, powered cart
- Swimming, slow treading
- Gardening or pruning
- Bicycling, very light effort
- Dusting or vacuuming
- Conditioning exercise, light stretching, or warm up

Moderate-Intensity Activities:

- Walking briskly
- Golf, pulling or carrying clubs

- Swimming, recreational

- Mowing lawn, power motor

- Tennis, doubles

- Bicycling 5–9 mph, level terrain, or with a few hills

- Scrubbing floors or washing windows

- Weight lifting, Nautilus machines or free weights

Vigorous-Intensity Activities:

- Racewalking, jogging, or running

- Swimming laps

- Mowing lawn, hand mower

- Tennis, singles

- Bicycling more than 10 mph, or on steep uphill terrain

- Moving or pushing furniture

- Circuit training

You may refer to Ainsworth, B. E., Haskell, W. L., Leon, A. S., et al. (1993). Compendium of physical activities: Classification of energy costs of human physical activities. *Medicine and Science in Sports and Exercise*, 25(1), 71–80; and Borg, G. (1998), *Perceived exertion and pain scales*, Champaign (IL): Human Kinetics, for more information in this regard.

How Much? How Fast?

The right amount of activity for a given individual depends upon the amount of activity the person is used to. "Moderate intensity" is actually a relative term and depends very much upon the person's level of fitness and cardiac conditioning. To be safe, it is strongly recommended that you purchase or borrow a heart rate monitor. The formula for calculating a safe heart rate is as follows:

Maximum heart rate $= 210-$ (your age)

A sedentary person who is not used to exercising should not exceed 60% of maximum heart rate. A fitter person who is accustomed to exercising can work at 80% of maximum heart rate. For example, a sedentary 60-year-old should not go above 90 beats per minute on a brisk walk.

Try wearing the heart rate monitor a few times during the coming week. Practice reading the monitor and seeing how your heart rate varies depending upon what you are doing. Be sure to bring the heart rate monitor to wear during next week's group walk.

When?

The activity program will begin next week. Your group will meet and walk once per week. Your group leader will work with you to establish a schedule for the walking program. Your group may choose to schedule the walk before or after your weekly session. Other times are possible, though. Work together with your group leader and the other members of your group to find a time that works for everyone.

You and your group will walk at a brisk pace—fast enough to cover a mile in 15 or 20 min. If you are an active person, you may already be able to walk briskly for 30 min. If you are unable to do so, it is recommended that you walk for 10–15 min several times throughout the rest of the week. This will help build your stamina.

In addition to bringing a heart rate monitor on the day of the group walk, you should also bring walking shoes, comfortable clothes, and white athletic socks, as these are designed to minimize blistering and rashes due to colored dyes. Your socks should comfortably fit the foot, with no excess material at the toe or heel to reduce the likelihood of blisters.

The Meal Replacement Plan

For homework last week, you were asked to compute your ideal calorie intake based upon your height, weight, and usual activity level. You will use this calorie estimate to order the foods you need from the meal replacement program your group is using. Your group leader will provide you with detailed information on the program, including instructions for ordering meals.

The major reason why most people gain weight after quitting smoking is that they eat more. The purpose of the meal replacement plan is to ensure that you haven't and won't increase your eating. The benefits of following a meal replacement plan include not needing to weigh or measure foods, estimate portion sizes, make nutritionally balanced selections, or count calories. The plan does all of that for you. If you stick to the plan, you will stay healthy; and you won't be hungry and you won't gain weight. Remember though, this program is not about losing weight. The main focus is to become a nonsmoker while maintaining your current weight. We strongly recommend that you do not try to lose weight until after you have successfully completed this program.

Why Use a Meal Replacement Plan?

The main reason for using the meal replacement program is to keep things simple. At this point in the program, you still need to devote full attention to staying smoke-free. Monitoring temptations to smoke while learning about nutrients, calories, and portion sizes is just too complicated. To simplify the task of weight management, the meal replacement plan regulates calories and provides you with nutritionally balanced, portion-controlled foods.

How Does the Meal Replacement Plan Work?

Each member of your group has estimated the number of calories she will need to maintain her body weight. The calorie estimate is based on each member's height, weight, and usual activity level. The estimate also reflects a reduction of 150 calories, to make up for the slowing of metabolism that happens as a result of withdrawing the metabolic boost produced by nicotine. The meal replacement plan allows you to select from a variety of meals and snack foods that lets you eat the right amount of calories in a low-fat, nutritionally balanced program. You will remain on the meal plan for 8 weeks (starting next week), until you are a confident, sure-footed nonsmoker. Then, you will gradually shift over to your own prepared foods

Most meal replacement programs are designed for weight loss. They supply 1200–1500 calories and incorporate very low fat foods. Since you are following a higher calorie, weight maintaining plan, you may feel that you are being supplied with and asked to eat a copious volume of food. It is important to eat the allotted amount, however. Do not skimp on meals! A well-balanced diet will keep you from getting hungry, and hunger is what leads to binging and overeating.

Daily Diary

Now that you are well on your way to becoming a nonsmoker, it is no longer necessary to fill out Pack-Wraps. Instead, you will begin tracking your daily habits using the Daily Diary. Use this form to track cigarettes smoked (if you happen to slip), alcohol consumed, and the day, time, and duration of your physical activity. The last column is for tracking your eating episodes and the calories consumed at each episode. You will begin filling out this column next week, once you begin the meal replacement plan. A blank copy of the diary can be found at the end of the chapter. Additional copies are provided in an appendix at the end of the book.

Homework (5 min)

- Make sure to place your order with the meal replacement program so the food arrives by next week.

- Begin using the Daily Diary to track your habits. Now that you are no longer smoking, you do not need to complete Pack-Wraps.

- Remember to practice wearing and reading the heart rate monitor. Bring the monitor and comfortable walking clothes to next week's meeting (if that's when your group takes a walk together).

Daily Diary

Day	No. of Cigarettes Smoked	Activity (type and minutes)	Meals or Snacks Calories Consumed	Alcohol Intake
Mon				
Tue				
Wed				
Thurs				
Fri				
Sat				
Sun				

Chapter 10   *Session 8*

Goals

- To continue relapse prevention planning
- To begin the physical activity program (group walk) and meal replacement plan

Relapse Prevention Planning

By now, you should have a good appreciation of the major relapse risks that concern you. This week, you will continue to learn how to manage these risks. Examples of factors that can lead to relapse are discussed in the sections that follow.

Major Stress

Major stressors in the areas of your relationships or job can trigger a relapse to smoking. It is understandable to feel threatened when trouble emerges in your life. In the past, smoking was probably your way of coping with the stress. As a new nonsmoker, you may find that when faced with a stress your thinking tends to go something like this: "This is a major crisis. One cigarette will help me get through it." It is important to be aware of these types of thoughts. Preparing an emergency response toolkit can help you deal with stress without resorting to smoking. In times of great temptation to smoke, visualize yourself reaching into your toolkit. The toolkit should be equipped with coping responses that you can grab and use instead of smoking. Here are some examples of response tools to include in your kit:

- Call a friend
- Go for a walk

- Practice deep breathing

- Chew a piece of gum

- Take a moment to think instead of reacting right away

All of these responses can make the difference between staying smoke-free and lighting up again. If one tool fails, reach into the toolbox again and grab another.

In the space provided, write a list of coping responses to include in your toolkit.

My Toolkit

1. _____

2. _____

3. _____

4. _____

5. _____

6. _____

7. _____

8. _____

9. _____

10. _____

Anger

Recent nonsmokers often have a lot of difficulty managing angry feelings. Their first impulse when they get mad may be to smoke a cigarette. In the heat of a furious moment, they may even feel that if they don't light up, they have no alternative except to become physically aggressive. Anger is another stressor that responds well to a toolkit that is prepared carefully and in advance. If anger is a problem for you, be on the lookout for scenarios that threaten a blow-up. Pack your toolkit with responses similar to those used to cope with the stressors discussed previously (e.g., call a friend or go for a walk) Doing something physically active is an especially good way to burn off angry feelings.

Special Occasions

It is not unusual for special occasions, such as holidays, anniversaries, vacations, or weddings to inspire a relapse. When you are having a really good time, you may feel that you "deserve a break." Even though this may be true, you need to be vigilant enough to recognize that smoking a cigarette is not the "break" you are looking for. You can treat yourself well in other ways that are not hazardous to your health.

Starting the Meal Replacement Plan

Starts Today—What to Eat

Since you placed your order last week, you should have already received your food from the meal replacement plan. You will start the plan with your next meal, following today's session. It is very important for you to eat all of your meal plan foods, even though it may seem like a lot. Doing so will ensure that you do not get very hungry, because hunger can trigger out-of-control binge eating.

Temptations to Overeat

Many of the same concepts that you have been using to manage your smoking can now be applied to managing your eating. Remember how you learned to be on the lookout for temptations to smoke? Now you should also be on the lookout for temptations to eat foods that are not on the meal plan. In fact, many of the stimuli that once triggered the urge to smoke may now trigger the urge to eat.

The best approach to keep eating and weight under control is to prevent slips. Like smoking slips, eating slips are like forest fires. It is best if they don't happen at all, and we do everything possible to prevent them, because that makes things easier. However, if a slip occurs, we do our best to contain it, and then learn from it so it doesn't happen again.

Alcohol

Now you have even more reasons to avoid drinking alcohol. Not only does getting tipsy diminish self-control over smoking, it can also result in overeating and poor food choices. Moreover, alcoholic beverages pack a powerful dose of calories. Alcohol is as calorically dense as fat. If others around you insist on drinking alcohol, order yourself a tonic, seltzer, or a virgin cocktail or non-alcoholic beer.

Going Out to Eat

Although it may be difficult, it is strongly recommended that you avoid eating out, especially early on in the meal plan, just because it makes things harder. If eating out is unavoidable, there are things you can do to ensure that you don't stray from the meal replacement plan. One is to bring your meal replacement food to the restaurant and ask the waiter to heat it up. You may feel uncomfortable doing this, but rest assured that you are not the first person to request it. Alternatively, you can order a small portion of grilled fish or chicken or a salad, with dressing on the side.

Going to a Barbecue or a Party

Partying that's associated with food is also discouraged at the start of the weight management portion of the program. If the event is unavoidable (like a holiday), try eating before the event or bring your own food. If neither is possible, you should avoid certain foods, such as salad dressings, tuna or macaroni salads with lots of mayo, avocado dips, olives, nuts, sour cream, or rich desserts.

Food Cravings

Like cigarette cravings, food cravings tend to be cued automatically, often by triggers that are outside of awareness. Try to figure out what triggers your cravings (i.e., a certain time, place, people, or emotion.) If you can learn when your food cravings tend to occur, you can plan a snack for that time. If you don't have a snack from the meal replacement program, water or diet beverages, rice cakes, gelatin, or salad vegetables substitute nicely.

The best thing about cravings is that they pass quickly. If you can distract yourself by engaging in a different activity, you will usually find that your food craving goes away.

Emotional Eating

Upset emotions are a problematic trigger for overeating, just as they are for smoking. Add strategies to your toolkit to deal with negative emotions that trigger an urge to eat. Many coping strategies already in the toolkit can be helpful, such as engaging in a physical activity or calling a friend for support. You may also consider journaling as a way to deal with strong emotions.

Monitoring Food and Alcohol Intake

Now that you are ready to begin the meal plan, you should start monitoring your eating. The Daily Diary form introduced last week has a column for tracking your diet. Be sure to complete this form on a daily basis over the course of the next week. You can find additional copies of the diary in an appendix at the end of the book. If you need extras, you may make photocopies.

The Physical Activity Program

The physical activity program begins today. Review the following points about the benefits of physical activity.

- Physical activity can reduce symptoms of nicotine withdrawal, including irritability, depression, insomnia, and cravings.

- Because activity enhances well-being and relaxation, it can become rewarding and offer you another form of gratification besides smoking or eating.

- Physical activity prevents metabolism from slowing down when nicotine is withdrawn, and thus helps to prevent weight gain.

- Finally, regular physical activity is one of the best known predictors of not gaining weight.

Also review the following points about the recommended amount of physical activity:

- Every American should engage in 30 min of moderate-intensity activity at least 5 days per week, preferably daily.

- Activity doesn't have to mean exercise. There are lots of enjoyable activities that can be done at moderate intensity. Refer back to the activities list in Chapter 9. There are also lots of small lifestyle changes that can increase activity (e.g., using the stairs instead of the elevator or parking further away from your destination so you have to walk).

- It isn't necessary to do 30 min of brisk activity all at once. You may need to build up to that amount.

- When you don't have the time, stamina, or desire to do 30 minutes of continuous activity, accumulate 10–15 min bouts throughout the day.

- At the very least, cut down on the amount of time that you spend in sedentary "screen time" pastimes, like watching television or using e-mail.

Remember to keep tracking your physical activity on the Daily Diary. Record the time spent engaging in all brisk activities lasting 10 min or more.

Group Walk

Today marks the start of the weekly group walk. As discussed last week, you and the members of your group will walk together at a brisk pace for approximately 15–20 min. Remember to wear your heart rate monitor and check it regularly to ensure that you are working within your target heart range.

Homework

✎ Begin the meal replacement plan using the foods you received this week.

✎ Begin the physical activity program.

✎ Remember to order your meal replacement foods for next week.

✎ Continue completing the Daily Diary.

✎ Remember to bring a heart rate monitor and walking clothes to the next session.

Chapter 11   *Session 9*

Goals

- To review your completed Daily Diaries to see how things are going, not only with smoking, but with your eating habits and physical activity as well

- To continue relapse prevention planning

- To participate in the group walk, if scheduled

Daily Diary Review

Although you have started the meal and activity components of the program, the main focus is still on staying smoke-free. Don't lose sight of this. Review your completed Daily Diaries with the group and discuss how things are going with tobacco abstinence. It is hoped that by now you are beginning to feel more secure as a nonsmoker. You should also be getting used to the meal and activity plans.

Relapse Prevention Planning

As in previous weeks, a major part of today's meeting will focus on relapse prevention. This week, it will take the form of a general group discussion. You will talk to the other members of your group about the successes and challenges you have been facing and the strategies you have been using to overcome any urges to smoke. If you are still struggling and experiencing slips, do not let it get you down. You are exhibiting tremendous courage in continuing with the program. Your group leader will help you anticipate and plan for difficult situations that might tempt smoking during the upcoming week.

How Are the Meal and Physical Activity Plans Going?

Your group leader will facilitate a brief discussion about the meal and activity plans and how you and the other members of your group are faring. Refer back to your completed Daily Diaries and ensure that you have been following the eating plan, minimizing your alcohol intake, and engaging in the recommended amount of physical activity.

The Meal Plan

One issue that some people may have with the meal plan is how to handle eating as a family. Some women will cook separate foods for the rest of the family while eating meal plan foods themselves. In other households, a different family member may take over food preparation temporarily. In any event, the family unit can continue to sit down together to share meals. It often happens that others in the household become intrigued by and interested in eating some of the meal replacement foods. If so, you can order additional meal replacement foods for them. Alternatively, you can encourage your family's interest in healthy eating so that the entire household can join when you eventually transition back to eating grocery store foods.

The Physical Activity Plan

Are you having an easy or hard time incorporating 30 min of physical activity into your daily routine? Discuss your thoughts with the other group members. Remember, you may engage in physical activity at any time of day that suits you. Check your neighborhood resources for opportunities to become active (walking groups, bike trails, etc.) Try to make activity part of your daily routine and involve others in being active.

Group Walk

If scheduled, you and the members of your group will walk together at a brisk pace for approximately 15–20 min. Remember to wear your heart rate monitor and check it regularly to ensure that you are working within your target heart range.

Homewok

✎ Continue participating in the meal and physical activity plans.

✎ Remember to order your meal replacement foods for next week.

✎ Continue completing the Daily Diary.

✎ Remember to bring a heart rate monitor and walking clothes to the next session.

Chapter 12 | *Session 10*

Goals

- To continue relapse prevention planning
- To review your completed Daily Diaries and check on progress with meal and activity plans
- To participate in the group walk, if scheduled

Relapse Prevention Planning

By this time, you and your group will have a good understanding of both shared and unique factors that interfere with abstinence. Today's discussion will focus on these factors and how to manage them.

Lapse versus Relapse

As you have been learning, a lapse is not the same as a relapse. A lapse or a slip can be contained and can teach a lesson about an area in which your coping needs to be improved. A slip is the signal to say, "Whoa! I don't want to waste my investment by having to quit all over again." Celebrate your investment by making a recommitment to stay smoke-free. As you already know, practice makes perfect

Dangerous Situations

Now that you are feeling more confident as a nonsmoker, you may find yourself taking certain risks. For example, you may allow a friend to smoke in your home or your car, or you may think about "having just one." These types of situations can trigger an urge to smoke so strong that it overpowers your will to resist smoking. You need to be cautious and not place yourself in situations that are beyond your skill level.

Coping With Feelings

As discussed a few weeks ago, you may have used smoking to alleviate strong feelings such as boredom, frustration, anger, etc. You will discuss with the group the feelings you have been experiencing and how you have been managing them without smoking.

How Are the Meal and Physical Activity Plans Going?

Similar to last week, your group leader will facilitate a brief discussion about the meal and activity plans and how you and the other members of your group are faring. Refer back to your completed Daily Diaries and ensure that you have been following the eating plan, minimizing your alcohol intake, and engaging in the recommended amount of physical activity.

Group Walk

If scheduled, you and the members of your group will walk together at a brisk pace for approximately 15–20 min. Remember to wear your heart rate monitor and check it regularly to ensure that you are working within your target heart range.

Homework

✎ Continue participating in the meal and physical activity plans.

✎ Remember to order your meal replacement foods for next week.

✎ Continue completing the Daily Diary.

✎ Remember to bring a heart rate monitor and walking clothes to the next session.

Chapter 13   *Session 11*

Goals

- To continue relapse prevention planning

- To begin incorporating pleasant events into your life

- To review your completed Daily Diaries and check on progress with meal and activity plans

- To participate in the group walk, if scheduled

Relapse Prevention Planning

It is important for you to be on the lookout for self-testing or risk-taking that could bring on a relapse. As mentioned last week, it is dangerous to take risks such as letting a friend smoke in your home or car, or to take a "drag" off of someone else's cigarette. Discuss with the group any dangerous or high-risk situations you may face in the upcoming week and plan strategies for handling them without smoking.

Scheduling Pleasant Events

You have been working hard to quit smoking and not gain weight. Giving up cigarettes can feel depriving, so it is important to find ways to preserve pleasure in your life. You deserve to treat yourself well. Following is a list of everyday pleasures that can be easily accessed and that most people enjoy. See whether you can find a way to experience at least one of these every day.

Pleasant Events

1. Explore someplace new	21. Light candles
2. Attend a lecture	22. Get a pedicure
3. Defend someone	23. Go sightseeing
4. Do things with children	24. See a play
5. Work in the garden	25. Play a board game
6. Discuss a special interest	26. Read a magazine
7. Get together with friends	27. Play an instrument
8. Collect natural objects	28. Sew or knit
9. Give or receive a massage	29. Sing
10. Do a jigsaw puzzle	30. Hug or kiss someone
11. Enjoy erotica (books, movies)	31. Listen to music
12. Buy something for yourself	32. Sit in the sun
13. Take a boat ride	33. Dress up
14. Call an old friend	34. Plan a trip
15. Take a steam shower	35. Visit a museum
16. Buy fresh flowers	36. Take photographs
17. Write a poem	37. Play cards
18. Have a picnic	38. Walk by a lake
19. Go fishing	39. Read something funny
20. Do arts and crafts	38. Play with an animal

How Are the Meal and Physical Activity Plans Going?

Similar to last week, your group leader will facilitate a brief discussion about the meal and activity plans and how you and the other members of your group are faring. Refer back to your completed Daily Diaries and ensure that you have been following the eating plan, minimizing your alcohol intake, and engaging in the recommended amount of physical activity.

Group Walk

If scheduled, you and the members of your group will walk together at a brisk pace for approximately 15–20 min. Remember to wear your heart rate monitor and check it regularly to ensure that you are working within your target heart range.

Homework

✎ Continue participating in the meal and physical activity plans.

✎ Remember to order your meal replacement foods for next week.

✎ Continue completing the Daily Diary.

✎ Remember to bring a heart rate monitor and walking clothes to the next session.

Chapter 14 *Session 12*

Goals

- To continue relapse prevention planning

- To add variety to your physical activity routine

- To begin preparing for transition off of the meal replacement program

- To participate in the group walk, if scheduled

Relapse Prevention Planning

Similar to the last several weeks, the first part of today's group discussion will center on relapse prevention planning. Your group leader will assist you and the other members of your group in problem solving and developing strategies to manage the triggers that interfere with you remaining a nonsmoker.

You will also review your completed Daily Diaries and discuss with the group how the meal and physical activity plans are going.

Spicing Up Your Activity Routine

By now you will be in the habit of being physically active nearly every day. To maintain your new healthier lifestyle, you may want to build some variety into your activity routine. Following is a list of different kinds of physically active pastimes that you can try out. You may find that some variety adds spice to your activity routine.

Physical Activities

1. Jogging
2. Aerobics
3. Swimming
4. Yoga
5. Walking
6. Golf
7. Dancing
8. Skiing
9. Bicycling
10. Climbing stairs
11. Hiking
12. Tennis
13. Basketball
14. Judo/Karate/Tae Kwan Do
15. Ice skating
16. Volleyball
17. Lifting weights
18. Exercise videotapes or DVDs
19. Racquetball
20. Playing catch
21. Badminton
22. Bowling
23. Playing tag
24. Climbing
25. Rowing

26. Chopping wood

27. Moving furniture

28. Rollerblading

Planning for Meal Plan Transition

This is your last week of eating meal replacements every day. Beginning next week, you will begin to slowly transition back to your own prepared (store-purchased) foods. You will start this transition by eating your own foods 1 day next week (week 13), 2 days the following week (week 14), 4 days the next week (week 15), and all 7 days in the next week (post-treatment).

You should begin to think about which day next week you will eat your own foods. Deciding on the day ahead of time will enable you to plan your choices.

Group Walk

If scheduled, you and the members of your group will walk together at a brisk pace for approximately 15–20 min. Remember to wear your heart rate monitor and check it regularly to ensure that you are working within your target heart range.

Homework

✎ Continue participating in the meal and physical activity plans.

✎ Remember to order your meal replacement foods for next week.

✎ Choose a day next week when you will eat off the meal replacement plan.

✎ Continue completing the Daily Diary.

✎ Remember to bring a heart rate monitor and walking clothes to the next session.

Chapter 15   *Session 13*

Goals

- To continue relapse prevention planning

- To begin discussion of energy balance

- To learn how to eat 1 day off the meal replacement plan

- To participate in the group walk, if scheduled

Relapse Prevention Planning

As usual, the first part of the session will be used to discuss relapse prevention. Your group leader will assist you and the other members of your group in problem solving and developing strategies to manage any remaining triggers that interfere with remaining a nonsmoker.

You will also review your completed Daily Diaries and discuss with the group how the meal and physical activity plans are going.

Planning for Meal Plan Transition

This week you will begin to transition off of the meal replacement program. Make sure that you have picked a day on which you will prepare your own meals.

You may be worried about gaining weight after discontinuing the use of the meal replacement plan. You may be asking yourself, "How am I going to decide what to eat?" Having followed a meal replacement plan for several weeks already has taught you many things about making smart food choices. You have learned healthy eating by eating healthily.

The following are helpful hints that you can use to help maintain your weight, without needing to make excessive behavioral changes.

Three Meals per Day

Eating on the meal replacement plan will have gotten you into the habit of eating three meals per day. This will help prevent weight gain as you transition back to choosing your own foods. It is very important that you refrain from skipping meals as a way to cut calories. Skipping meals is a very common, yet ill-advised strategy to try to control body weight. The approach usually fails because it allows you to become hungry, which leaves you vulnerable to eating temptations. If you skip meals, you will likely end up overeating or bingeing when you finally do eat.

Portion Control

Eating meal replacement foods has exposed you to portion sizes that are consistent with healthy eating. Although it seemed as though you were eating more than usual, your portion sizes were actually much smaller than those of the meals you were accustomed to eating previously. By now, you should be used to eating smaller portions. Portion control is an excellent habit to preserve as you transition back to choosing your own foods. It may be helpful to use smaller plates, which make portions visually appear larger.

Calorie Regulation

Maintaining body weight is a straightforward matter of energy balance. To not gain weight, a person needs to expend as much energy (calories) as they take in. Unfortunately, most ways of intentionally burning calories (e.g., by exercising) are inefficient compared to how easily calories are taken in. Think of how quickly and easily you can eat a candy bar that supplies 300 calories, and compare that to the 45–60 min you need to spend on the treadmill to work off those calories. Be sure to review your daily calorie intake and observe how you distribute your intake across the day.

Planning Your Day Off Meal Replacement

Different women choose to eat differently on their first day off the meal replacement program. Some prefer to eat very similarly to how they eat on the meal replacement plan; only they substitute foods purchased from the grocery store. Others prefer to transition back to preparing their own foods "from scratch." Either approach works fine; the choice just depends on what feels right for you. To help choose what to eat on your "day off," you can consult Table 15.1, which shows prepackaged grocery store foods that resemble those you have been eating as meal replacements. Alternatively, you can search for recipes in one of the low-calorie, low-fat cookbooks listed in Table 15.2 at the end of this section. The most important thing is to plan ahead for what you will eat on your day off. That way, you won't find yourself at the complete mercy of whatever is in your kitchen cabinets or at the nearby fast food restaurant.

Group Walk

If scheduled, you and the members of your group will walk together at a brisk pace for approximately 15–20 min. Remember to wear your heart rate monitor and check it regularly to ensure that you are working within your target heart range.

Table 15.1 Low-Calorie Prepackaged Meal Items

Breakfast
Cheerios (with 1/2 cup milk)
Raisin Bran (with 1/2 cup milk)
Wheaties (with 1/2 cup milk)
Instant oatmeal
Small plain bagel with fat-free cream cheese

Lunch
Fantastic soup cup
Healthy Choice soup bowl
Healthy Choice or Lean Cuisine panini
Amy's pizza
Amy's burrito
Yogurt, fruit, low-fat with low-calorie sweetener

Dinner
Healthy Choice Complete Selections or Café Steamers
Lean Cuisine Café Classics, Comfort Classics, or Spa Cuisine
Weight Watchers Smart Ones
Amy's frozen dinner

Note: Supplement these meal items with skim milk, fresh fruit, and vegetables to reach recommended calories.

Table 15.2 Low-Calorie, Low-Fat Cookbooks

Title	Author
Low-Calorie Cookbook	American Heart Association
Low-Fat, Low-Cholesterol Cookbook	American Heart Association
Healthy Cooking for Two (or Just You)	Francis Price
Cooking Light: Low Fat, Low Calorie	Leisure Arts
The 1200–Calorie-a-Day Menu Cookbook	Nancy S. Hughes
Low Calorie Cookbook	Readers Digest Editors
Secrets of Fat-Free Cooking	Sandra Woodruff
The Good Morning America Cut the Calories Cookbook	Sara Moulton, Jean Anderson, Emeril Lagasse
The Complete Cooking Light Cookbook	Cathy A. Wesler
Cooking Light Superfast Suppers	Anne C. Cain
2008 CalorieKing Calorie, Fat, and Carbohydrate Counter	Allan Borushek
Weight Watchers New Complete Cookbook	Weight Watchers
Rachael Ray's 30-Minute Get Real Meals	Rachael Ray

Homework

✎ Continue participating in the meal and physical activity plans, but plan to select your own calorie-equivalent foods 1 day this coming week.

✎ Remember to order your meal replacement foods for next week.

✎ Continue completing the Daily Diary.

✎ Remember to bring a heart rate monitor and walking clothes to the next session.

Chapter 16   *Session 14*

Goals

- To continue relapse prevention planning

- To plan how to eat 2 days off the meal replacement plan

- To participate in group walk, if scheduled

Relapse Prevention Planning

The first part of the session will continue the group's discussion of relapse prevention. You will work with your group leader to solve problems and develop strategies to manage any lingering barriers that interfere with remaining smoke-free.

You will also review your completed Daily Diaries and discuss with the group how the meal and physical activity plans are going.

Planning for Meal Plan Transition

Two days this week you will eat off the meal replacement plan. You should know which 2 days you will do this and what you are going to eat. Refer back to the energy balance information in the previous chapter for more information.

The following are additional helpful hints that you can use to help maintain your weight.

Limit Fat Intake

Fats contain twice the calories of carbohydrates and proteins. You are encouraged to use fat-free dressing; avoid mayo-filled chicken or tuna salads; cut back on usage of butter and margarine. In addition, you may consider using meat as a "condiment," i.e., adding meat in small quantities to dishes that include many vegetables (e.g., salads or stir fried dishes). If you enjoy eating meat, try choosing chicken (without the skin) and fish instead of ribs, pork chops, and beef. Ground turkey can be substituted for beef or you can eat beef in small portions and choose cuts that are lower in fat content (e.g., sirloin, tenderloin, round steak, 80–90% fat-free ground beef). Deep-fried foods (e.g., French fries, donuts, onion rings) should be avoided if possible. Also, even though foods like nuts and avocados contain the healthiest kinds of fats (polyunsaturated, monounsaturated), you should eat them in only limited quantities because of their high calorie content. Review the information that follows:

Fat Gram Counting

An easy way to keep track of your calorie intake is to count the number of fat grams you consume each day. It is recommended that for a healthy diet, fat intake should be between 25 and 30% of your total daily calories. Rather than figuring percentages of fat to total calories, we have provided you with the following table that lists various calorie levels and the number of fat grams associated with each. To figure out the number of fat grams in your diet you only have to find your calorie level. For example, if you are on a 1,650-calorie meal plan, your fat gram intake should be between 46 and 55 g each day.

Calorie Level	Number of Fat Grams
1,200	33–40
1,500	42–50
1,650	46–55
1,800	50–60
1,950	54–65
2,100	58–70
2,250	63–75
2,400	67–80

The following section lists common food items and their fat content.

Food Items	Number of Fat Grams
Beef (about the size of a deck of cards)	
3 oz ground	17.7
3 oz sirloin steak	16.0
3 oz rib, large end (6 inches)	27.7
Pork (about the size of a deck of cards)	
3 oz loin	23.3
3 oz spareribs (6 inches)	25.7
Lamb (about the size of a deck of cards)	
3 oz leg	16.1
1 loin chop	20.9
Chicken (about the size of a deck of cards)	
Half skinless breast	3.1
Half breast with skin	7.6
1 drumstick	5.8
Turkey (about the size of a half a deck of cards)	
1 oz breast	0.7
1 oz drumstick	2.4
Fish (about the size of a deck of cards)	
3 oz haddock or cod	0.6
3 oz shrimp	1.5
3 oz lobster	0.8
1 fish stick	3.4
Cheese (about 1 slice)	
1 oz American, processed	8.9
1 oz cheddar	8.4
1 oz Colby	9.1
1 oz Swiss	7.8
Eggs	
1 hard boiled	5.1
1 fried	5.6
1 scrambled	5.8
Fruits and Vegetables (most fruits and vegetables have less than 1 g of fat)	
Salad Dressings (1 tbsp each)	
French	0.9
Italian	1.5
Russian	0.7
Thousand Island	1.6
Blue cheese	8.0

continued

continued

Food Items	Number of Fat Grams
Condiments (1 tbsp each)	
Butter	11.5
80% fat margarine	11.4
60% fat margarine	8.6
40% fat margarine	5.5
Mayonnaise	10.9
Lard	12.8
Beverages (1 cup)	
8 oz 1% low-fat milk	2.6
8 oz 2% low-fat milk	4.7
8 oz skim milk	0.4
8 oz frozen orange juice	0.1
8 oz fresh orange juice	0.5
8 oz apple juice	0.3
6 oz tomato juice	0.1

To find the fat content of other foods, visit www.calorieking.com/mobile/, which gives the fat and calorie content of 50,000 foods free of charge.

Dairy Selection

Dairy products are good sources of protein, but they can also be very high in calories. If possible, select skim or 1% milk instead of whole milk or cream. Many cheeses are very high in fat, so it is wise to limit the amount of cheese or select lower-fat cheeses such as feta, cottage cheese, or part-skim mozzarella. Choose sugar-free, low-fat yogurts. When cooking, substitute egg whites (17 calories!) for most egg yolks.

Increase Intake of Fruits and Vegetables

Rest assured you don't have to cut back on everything. You can actually increase your intake of fruits and vegetables. Generally, fruits and vegetables are lower in calories and fat than other foods (exceptions include avocados, coconuts, and nuts). Fruits and vegetables make excellent snacks and are great a source of natural fiber and vitamins. If you are looking for some ideas about new fruits or vegetables to try, check the following list.

- Oranges
- Tomatoes
- Broccoli
- Apples
- Carrots
- Bananas
- Green beans
- Green peas
- Raisins
- Strawberries
- Cucumbers
- Sweet potatoes
- Cantaloupe
- Corn
- Acorn or butternut squash
- Grapefruit
- Grapes
- Pineapple

- Cauliflower
- Cherries
- Radishes
- Mushrooms
- Peppers
- Watermelon
- Blueberries
- Beets
- Spinach
- Honeydew melon
- Raspberries
- Plums
- Pears
- Bean sprouts
- Asparagus
- Celery
- Blackberries
- Nectarines

Group Walk

If scheduled, you and the members of your group will walk together at a brisk pace for approximately 15–20 min. Remember to wear your heart rate monitor and check it regularly to ensure that you are working within your target heart range.

Homework

✎ Continue participating in the meal and physical activity plans, but plan to select your own calorie-equivalent foods on 2 days this coming week.

✎ Remember to order your meal replacement foods for next week.

✎ Continue completing the Daily Diary.

✎ Remember to bring a heart rate monitor and walking clothes to the next session.

Chapter 17   *Session 15*

Goals

- To continue relapse prevention planning
- To plan how to eat 4 days off the meal replacement plan
- To participate in group walk, if scheduled

Relapse Prevention Planning

This will be your second to last treatment session. Your group leader will assist you in mastering any remaining smoking triggers. You and the other group members will clarify which potential pitfalls you need to watch for most vigilantly going forward.

You will also review your completed Daily Diaries and discuss with the group how the meal and physical activity plans are going.

Planning for Meal Plan Transition

Four days this week you will eat off the meal replacement plan. You should know which 4 days you will do this and what you are going to eat. Refer back to the energy balance concepts presented in the past 2 weeks for more information.

Food labels offer useful information that can help you maintain your weight. But they are not always easy to decipher. The following information about nutrition labels may help you.

Label Lingo

The food makers of America have conspired to confound and confuse the general public by developing their own lingo, which has made it impossible for the average person to make any sense out of food labels. With all the different terms appearing on nutrition labels these days, it is especially important for people to have an understanding of what these terms mean so they can make healthy and smart food choices when shopping. Never fear! The Food and Drug Administration (FDA) has issued guidelines that a food must meet before it can be labeled "low fat," "low calorie," etc.

If you are concerned about calories, fat, or weight management, look for the following terms on food labels:

Calorie-free	Fewer than 5 calories
Low-calorie	40 calories or fewer
Reduced calorie	At least 25% less calories than the regular product
Light or lite	One-third fewer calories or 50% less fat than the regular product; if more than half the calories are from fat, fat content must be reduced by 50% or more
Fat-free	Less than a 1/2 g of fat
Low-fat	3 g of fat or less
Reduced-fat	At least 25% less fat than the regular product
Cholesterol-free	Less than 2 mg cholesterol and 2 g or fewer of saturated fat
Low-cholesterol	20 mg or fewer cholesterol and 2 g or fewer saturated fat
Lean	Meat, poultry, seafood, and game meat with fewer than 10 g total fat, fewer than 4 g saturated fat, and fewer than 95 mg cholesterol per 100 g and per labeled serving. Main dish, meal, and meal-type products with fewer than 10 g total fat, fewer than 4 g saturated fat, and fewer than 95 mg cholesterol per 100 g and per labeled serving
Extra lean	Meat, poultry, seafood, and game meat with fewer than 5 g total fat, fewer than 2 g saturated fat, and fewer than 95 mg of cholesterol per labeled serving and per 100 g. Main dish, meal, and meal-type products with fewer than 5 g total fat, fewer than 2 g saturated fat, and fewer than 95 mg cholesterol per 100 g and per labeled serving

If you are interested in vitamins and minerals, some helpful terms include:

Good source	10–19% of daily value
Rich in	20% or more of the daily value. Also referred to as "excellent source of . . . "
Fortified or enriched	Contains at least 10% more than the daily value when compared to the reference food

If you are particularly concerned about sodium (salt), some helpful terms include:

Low sodium	140 mg or less sodium
Reduced sodium	At least 25% less sodium than the regular product

If you are concerned about carbohydrate (fiber and sugar) intake, watch for these terms:

Good source of fiber	3 to fewer than 5 g of fiber or 10–19% of the daily value for fiber
Excellent source of fiber	5 g or more of fiber or 20% of the daily value. Also called "high fiber."
Sugar-free	Less than 1/2 g of sugar
Reduced sugar	At least 25% less sugar than the regular product

So remember, don't be misled by fancy lingo. Read the labels!

Similar foods now have standardized serving sizes, making it easier to compare the nutrition values of foods and beverages.

Nutrition Facts

Serving Size ½ cup (114 g)
Servings Per Container 4

Amount Per Serving

Calories 90	Calories from Fat 30

	% Daily Value*
Total Fat 3 g	5%
Saturated Fat 0 g	0%
Cholesterol 0 mg	0%
Sodium 300 mg	13%
Total Carbohydrate 13 g	4%
Dietary Fiber 3 g	12%
Sugars 3 g	
Protein 3 g	

Vitamin A 80%	●	Vitamin C 60%
Calcium 4%	●	Iron 4%

The % Daily Value column shows how a serving of this food fits into a 2,000-calorie reference diet and helps you easily determine if a food contributes a lot or a little of a particular nutrient. Use % Daily Values as a guide to help you monitor your daily percentages of fat, saturated fat, cholesterol and sodium. For total carbohydrate, dietary fiber, vitamins and minerals, try to reach 100% of your daily value for each.

Recommended daily amounts of some nutrients for two reference diets (2,000 & 2,500 calories). Consult a registered dietitian to find out what your own nutrient needs are.

*Percent Daily Values are based on a 2,000-calorie diet. Your daily values may be higher or lower depending on your calorie needs:

		Calories	2,000	2,500
Total Fat	Less than		65 g	80 g
Sat Fat	Less than		20 g	25 g
Cholesterol	Less than		300 mg	300 mg
Sodium	Less than		2,400 mg	2,400 mg
Total Carbohydrate			300 mg	375 mg
Fiber			25 g	30 g

For more complete information on the new label and labeling regulations, contact the Food and Drug Administration's Consumer Affairs Department in writing at: 5600 Fishers Lane (HFE-88), Rockville, MD 20857. You can also contact your local or regional FDA public affairs specialists or Cooperative Extension Service educators listed in the blue pages of your phone book. In addition, a registered dietitian in your area can help answer your questions about the new label.

Figure 17.1

Nutrition label

Substitutes

Avoid or limit processed lunchmeats such as salami, bologna, and hot dogs. As an alternative, select sliced turkey or ham. Instead of sweetened sodas, substitute diet sodas or zero-calorie beverages. Instead of using butter or a cheese sauce, try using lemon for flavoring. Instead of choosing cakes or cookies for dessert, try substituting fruit. Review the following information regarding making healthy substitutions.

Dairy Products

Higher-Fat Foods	Lower-Fat Foods
✓ Evaporated whole milk	✓ Evaporated fat-free (skim) or reduced-fat (2%) milk
✓ Whole milk	✓ Low-fat (1%), reduced-fat (2%), or fat-free (skim) milk
✓ Ice cream	✓ Sorbet, sherbet, low-fat or fat-free frozen yogurt
✓ Whipped cream	✓ Imitation whipped cream (made with fat-free [skim] milk)
✓ Sour cream	✓ Plain low-fat yogurt
✓ Cream cheese	✓ Neufchatel or "light" cream cheese or fat-free cream cheese
✓ Cheese (cheddar, Swiss, jack)	✓ Reduced-calorie cheese, low-calorie processed cheeses, etc.
	✓ Fat-free cheese
✓ American cheese	✓ Fat-free American cheese or other types of fat-free cheeses
✓ Regular (4%) cottage cheese	✓ Low-fat (1%) or reduced-fat (2%) cottage cheese
✓ Whole milk mozzarella cheese	✓ Part-skim milk, low-moisture mozzarella cheese
✓ Whole milk ricotta cheese	✓ Part-skim milk ricotta cheese
✓ Coffee cream (half and half) or nondairy creamer (liquid, powder)	✓ Low-fat (1%) or reduced-fat (2%) milk or non-fat dry milk powder

Cereals, Grains, and Pastas

Higher-Fat Foods	Lower-Fat Foods
✓ Ramen noodles	✓ Rice or noodles (spaghetti, macaroni, etc.)
✓ Pasta with white sauce (alfredo)	✓ Pasta with red sauce (marinara)
✓ Pasta with cheese sauce	✓ Pasta with vegetables (primavera)
✓ Granola	✓ Bran flakes, crispy rice, etc.
	✓ Cooked grits or oatmeal
	✓ Reduced-fat granola

Meat, Fish, and Poultry

Higher-Fat Foods	Lower-Fat Foods
✓ Cold cuts or lunch meats (bologna, salami, liverwurst, etc.)	✓ Low-fat cold cuts (95–97% fat-free lunch meats, low-fat pressed meats)
✓ Hot dogs (regular)	✓ Lower-fat hot dogs
✓ Bacon or sausage	✓ Canadian bacon or lean ham
✓ Regular ground beef	✓ Extra-lean ground beef such as ground round or ground turkey (read labels)
✓ Chicken or turkey with skin, duck, or goose	✓ Chicken or turkey without skin (white meat)
✓ Oil-packed tuna	✓ Water-packed tuna (rinse to reduce sodium content)
✓ Beef (chuck, rib, brisket)	✓ Beef (round, loin) (trimmed of external fat)
✓ Pork (spareribs, untrimmed loin)	✓ Pork tenderloin or trimmed, lean smoked ham
✓ Frozen breaded fish or fried fish (homemade or commercial)	✓ Fish or shellfish, unbreaded (fresh, frozen, canned in water)
✓ Whole eggs	✓ Egg whites or egg substitutes
✓ Frozen TV dinners (containing more than 13 g of fat per serving)	✓ Frozen TV dinners (containing less than 13 g of fat per serving and lower in sodium)
✓ Chorizo sausage	✓ Turkey sausage, drained well (read label)
	✓ Vegetarian sausage (made with tofu)

Baked Goods

Higher-Fat Foods	Lower-Fat Foods
✓ Croissants, brioches, etc.	✓ Hard french rolls or soft brown 'n serve rolls
✓ Donuts, sweet rolls, muffins, scones, or pastries	✓ English muffins, bagels, reduced-fat or fat-free muffins or scones
✓ Party crackers	✓ Low-fat crackers (choose ones lower in sodium)
	✓ Saltine or soda crackers (choose ones lower in sodium)
✓ Cake (pound, chocolate, yellow)	✓ Cake (angel food, white, gingerbread)
✓ Cookies	✓ Reduced-fat or fat-free cookies (graham crackers, ginger snaps, fig bars) (compare calorie level)

Snacks and Sweets

Higher-Fat Foods	Lower-Fat Foods
✓ Nuts	✓ Popcorn (air-popped or light microwave), fruits, vegetables
✓ Ice cream, e.g., cones or bars	✓ Frozen yogurt, frozen fruit, or chocolate pudding bars
✓ Custards or puddings (made with whole milk)	✓ Puddings (made with skim milk)

Fats, Oils, and Salad Dressings

Higher-Fat Foods	Lower-Fat Foods
✓ Regular margarine or butter	✓ Light-spread margarines, diet margarine, or whipped butter, tub or squeeze bottle
✓ Regular mayonnaise	✓ Light or diet mayonnaise or mustard
✓ Regular salad dressings	✓ Reduced-calorie or fat-free salad dressings, lemon juice, or plain, herb-flavored, or wine vinegar
✓ Butter or margarine on toast or bread	✓ Jelly, jam, or honey on bread or toast
✓ Oils, shortening, or lard	✓ Nonstick cooking spray for stir-frying or sautéing
	✓ As a substitute for oil or butter, use applesauce or prune puree in baked goods

Miscellaneous

Higher-Fat Foods	**Lower-Fat Foods**
✓ Canned cream soups	✓ Canned broth-based soups
✓ Canned beans and franks	✓ Canned baked beans in tomato sauce
✓ Gravy (homemade with fat and/or milk)	✓ Gravy mixes made with water or homemade with the fat skimmed off and fat-free milk
✓ Fudge sauce	✓ Chocolate syrup
✓ Avocado on sandwiches	✓ Cucumber slices or lettuce leaves
✓ Guacamole dip or refried beans with lard	✓ Salsa

Healthy Snacks

You may find that you need a between-meal snack in the afternoon or evening. See the following list for ideas of different snacks with 100 calories or less.

Hard-boiled egg	1 cup turkey vegetable soup
1 cup raspberries	4 Brazil nuts
Stick of string cheese	1 ear of corn (plain)
10 animal crackers	1 cup unsweetened fruit cocktail
Red bell pepper with 3 tablespoons of hummus	2 shortbread cookies
Half of a medium cantaloupe	20 small cherries
1 handful (1 oz) fat-free pretzels	large pineapple slice
Frozen fruit bar	4 graham crackers
12 almonds	8 olives
Large dill pickle	4 marshmallows
Café latte with fat-free milk (8 oz)	1 slice toast and 1 tsp jelly
3 cups light microwave popcorn	6 Ritz crackers
Apple	2 tangerines
4 saltines	1 small pita
1 cup fat-free, sugar-free flavored yogurt	1 slice provolone cheese (1 oz)
1 cup minestrone soup	mango
1 tbsp peanut butter on a celery stalk	20 oyster crackers
2 ladyfingers	1/2 cup sherbet
2 oz turkey	1 container sugar-free pudding
1 cup tomato juice	1 piece beef jerky (.7 oz)
Medium pear	2 caramel corn rice cakes (.5 oz)
1/2 cup fat-free cottage cheese	1/2 cup fat-free frozen yogurt

1 cup beef barley soup	1/2 cup tuna (canned in water)
Small baked potato	Peach
1 cup blueberries	20 roasted peanuts
6 ginger snaps	Orange
4 large carrots	1/2 cup fat-free cottage cheese
12 radishes	Small banana
1 cup chicken noodle soup	4 oz shrimp
2 sesame breadsticks	4 stalks broccoli
60 gold fish crackers	4 apricots
1/2 English muffin and 1/2 tsp butter	25 pistachios
1 Milano cookie	2 kiwis
1 cup chicken rice soup	1/2 cup prune juice
10 walnut halves	1 cup skim milk
1 tortilla	1/2 cup oatmeal
5 Nabisco Nilla Wafers	60 Pepperidge Farm Baby Gold Fish Crackers
1 Yoplait Light Smoothie	9 Tootsie Roll Midgees
12 Quaker Oats Cheddar Cheese Rice Snacks	Mini bagel with 1 ounce of smoked salmon

Group Walk

If scheduled, you and the members of your group will walk together at a brisk pace for approximately 15–20 min. Remember to wear your heart rate monitor and check it regularly to ensure that you are working within your target heart range.

Homework

✎ Continue participating in the meal and physical activity plans, but plan to select your own calorie-equivalent foods on 4 days this coming week.

✎ Remember to order your meal replacement foods for next week.

✎ Continue completing the Daily Diary.

✎ Remember to bring a heart rate monitor and walking clothes to the next session.

Chapter 18   *Session 16*

Goals

- To meet with your group for a final time

- To look toward the future

This week marks the end of the smoking cessation program. It is hoped that by this point, you are feeling confident in your ability to resist smoking, manage your eating, and maintain a healthy, active lifestyle. You may have some trepidation about coping effectively on your own, without the support of your group and group leader. You and the other members of your group have shared and supported each other through a challenging experience. It is normal to experience some feelings of loss as the program ends. However, just because formal meetings are ending, it does not mean that you are entirely on your own. You should feel free to contact the other members of your group (or your group leader) for support as needed. Remember also that your group leader may conduct monthly follow-up sessions in order to help you keep up your progress.

Preventing Relapse

Now that the program is ending, it is even more important that you have an ironclad plan for preventing relapse. Remind yourself of the rewards of being smoke-free. Try to imagine any circumstance, temptation, or emotion that could cause you to slip in the future, and plan for how to cope effectively and manage your urges to smoke. An important step in preventing relapse is to begin to identify yourself as a nonsmoker.

Making Healthy and Smart Food Choices

As you know, managing your calorie intake is not an easy task, especially without the help of a meal replacement plan. Remember, you are not dieting to lose weight. Instead, you are eating healthful foods to maintain your weight and improve your cardiovascular and overall health.

In order to start you off on track with your weight maintenance program, we have provided you with a day's worth of healthy, low-fat recipes that you may wish to try. You can find many more recipes in the cookbooks mentioned in Chapter 15.

A Day of Low-Calorie Recipes

Berry Banana Breakfast Smoothie

Ingredients:

- 1 cup low-fat soy milk

- 1/2 cup water

- 1 medium banana—peeled, sliced, and frozen overnight in a freezer bag

- 1 cup frozen blueberries, raspberries, or peaches

- 1/2 teaspoon vanilla extract

Preparation:

Combine all ingredients in a blender and puree until smooth. Serve garnished with berries or banana slices

Serves 1

Gazpacho (Hot Weather Lunch)

Ingredients:

- 3 large tomatoes (peeled)

- 1 red bell pepper

- 1 medium cucumber

- 1/2 small purple onion

- 4 garlic cloves

- 1.5 slices of bread

- 1 cup water

- 1/2 teaspoon cumin

- 1/8 teaspoon paprika

- 4 tablespoons red wine

- 1 teaspoon salt

- 1/4 teaspoon ground black pepper, to taste

Preparation:

Chop the vegetables coarsely. Chop the garlic finely.

Put into a blender the mixed vegetables, bread, and water. Blend well but not to the point of completely pureeing (i.e., preserve some texture). Pour the blended contents into a bowl; whisk in the remaining ingredients. Refrigerate overnight before serving. Serve cold.

Serves 2

Stir-Fried Chicken With Asparagus, Water Chestnuts, and Black Bean Sauce

Ingredients:

- 1 lb boneless, skinless chicken breast (cut into bite-size pieces)

- 3 tbsp black bean sauce

- 1 tbsp peanut oil

- 1 fresh red chili, diced very finely

- 8 oz can sliced water chestnuts (rinse well in cold water)

- 12 asparagus spears sliced diagonally into 1.5-inch spears

Preparation:

Marinate chicken in black bean sauce for 15 min.

Heat the wok. Add the peanut oil. When the oil is very hot and begins to smoke, add the chili. Stir-fry for 30 seconds. Add the chicken and the black bean marinade. Keep stirring for 1 min. Add the water chestnuts and the asparagus. Stir fry 4–5 min or until the chicken is cooked through and the vegetables are cooked but still crisp.

Serves 4

Staying Physically Active

It is hoped that you have come to enjoy exercising and will want to continue with it. In order to avoid boredom, we encourage you to experiment with different types of activities, such as bicycling, swimming, yoga, Pilates, etc. Check your local YMCA or recreational center for upcoming events (e.g., hiking trips or sporting events).

The Future

Congratulations on becoming a nonsmoker! You have worked very hard to overcome your previous smoking habit and to do so in a way that also manages your weight effectively. Staying smoke-free in the future will not always be simple, but things will get easier over time.

Since practice makes perfect, you should always refer back to the techniques and strategies you learned to manage high-risk situations and urges to smoke. The changes that you have made have put you well on your way to a longer, healthier life. We wish you continued success!

Appendix of Forms

Assignment: Pack-Wraps

Wrap this daily cigarette count sheet around your pack of cigarettes and secure it with a rubber band. When you are about to take a cigarette, before you actually put it in your mouth and light up, indicate the following:

1) **Time of day**
2) **Activity you are involved in**
3) **Word/words that best describe your feeling at the time**
4) **How much do you need that particular cigarette:**

1 – Very Strongly Needed   **2 – Strongly Needed**   **3 – Weakly Needed**

# of Cigarette	Time	Food/Alcohol	Relaxation	Work	Social	Driving	Other (please describe)	Angry	Anxious	Bored	Depressed	Frustrated	Happy	Relaxed	Tired	Need Rating		
1																1	2	3
2																1	2	3
3																1	2	3
4																1	2	3
5																1	2	3
6																1	2	3
7																1	2	3
8																1	2	3
9																1	2	3
10																1	2	3
11																1	2	3
12																1	2	3
13																1	2	3
14																1	2	3
15																1	2	3
16																1	2	3
17																1	2	3
18																1	2	3
19																1	2	3
20																1	2	3

Assignment: Pack-Wraps

Wrap this daily cigarette count sheet around your pack of cigarettes and secure it with a rubber band. When you are about to take a cigarette, before you actually put it in your mouth and light up, indicate the following:

1) **Time of day**
2) **Activity you are involved in**
3) **Word/words that best describe your feeling at the time**
4) **How much do you need that particular cigarette:**

1 – Very Strongly Needed   2 – Strongly Needed   3 – Weakly Needed

# of Cigarette	Time	Food/Alcohol	Relaxation	Work	Social	Driving	Other (please describe)	Angry	Anxious	Bored	Depressed	Frustrated	Happy	Relaxed	Tired	Need Rating		
1																1	2	3
2																1	2	3
3																1	2	3
4																1	2	3
5																1	2	3
6																1	2	3
7																1	2	3
8																1	2	3
9																1	2	3
10																1	2	3
11																1	2	3
12																1	2	3
13																1	2	3
14																1	2	3
15																1	2	3
16																1	2	3
17																1	2	3
18																1	2	3
19																1	2	3
20																1	2	3

Assignment: Pack-Wraps

Wrap this daily cigarette count sheet around your pack of cigarettes and secure it with a rubber band. When you are about to take a cigarette, before you actually put it in your mouth and light up, indicate the following:

1) **Time of day**
2) **Activity you are involved in**
3) **Word/words that best describe your feeling at the time**
4) **How much do you need that particular cigarette:**

1 – Very Strongly Needed   **2 – Strongly Needed**   **3 – Weakly Needed**

# of Cigarette	Time	Food/Alcohol	Relaxation	Work	Social	Driving	Other (please describe)	Angry	Anxious	Bored	Depressed	Frustrated	Happy	Relaxed	Tired	Need Rating		
1																1	2	3
2																1	2	3
3																1	2	3
4																1	2	3
5																1	2	3
6																1	2	3
7																1	2	3
8																1	2	3
9																1	2	3
10																1	2	3
11																1	2	3
12																1	2	3
13																1	2	3
14																1	2	3
15																1	2	3
16																1	2	3
17																1	2	3
18																1	2	3
19																1	2	3
20																1	2	3

Assignment: Pack-Wraps

Wrap this daily cigarette count sheet around your pack of cigarettes and secure it with a rubber band. When you are about to take a cigarette, before you actually put it in your mouth and light up, indicate the following:

1) **Time of day**
2) **Activity you are involved in**
3) **Word/words that best describe your feeling at the time**
4) **How much do you need that particular cigarette:**

1 – **Very Strongly Needed**   2 – **Strongly Needed**   3 – **Weakly Needed**

# of Cigarette	Time	Food/Alcohol	Relaxation	Work	Social	Driving	Other (please describe)	Angry	Anxious	Bored	Depressed	Frustrated	Happy	Relaxed	Tired	Need Rating		
1																1	2	3
2																1	2	3
3																1	2	3
4																1	2	3
5																1	2	3
6																1	2	3
7																1	2	3
8																1	2	3
9																1	2	3
10																1	2	3
11																1	2	3
12																1	2	3
13																1	2	3
14																1	2	3
15																1	2	3
16																1	2	3
17																1	2	3
18																1	2	3
19																1	2	3
20																1	2	3

Assignment: Pack-Wraps

Wrap this daily cigarette count sheet around your pack of cigarettes and secure it with a rubber band. When you are about to take a cigarette, before you actually put it in your mouth and light up, indicate the following:

1) **Time of day**
2) **Activity you are involved in**
3) **Word/words that best describe your feeling at the time**
4) **How much do you need that particular cigarette:**

1 – Very Strongly Needed   2 – Strongly Needed   3 – Weakly Needed

# of Cigarette	Time	Food/Alcohol	Relaxation	Work	Social	Driving	Other (please describe)	Angry	Anxious	Bored	Depressed	Frustrated	Happy	Relaxed	Tired	Need Rating		
1																1	2	3
2																1	2	3
3																1	2	3
4																1	2	3
5																1	2	3
6																1	2	3
7																1	2	3
8																1	2	3
9																1	2	3
10																1	2	3
11																1	2	3
12																1	2	3
13																1	2	3
14																1	2	3
15																1	2	3
16																1	2	3
17																1	2	3
18																1	2	3
19																1	2	3
20																1	2	3

Assignment: Pack-Wraps

Wrap this daily cigarette count sheet around your pack of cigarettes and secure it with a rubber band. When you are about to take a cigarette, before you actually put it in your mouth and light up, indicate the following:

1) **Time of day**
2) **Activity you are involved in**
3) **Word/words that best describe your feeling at the time**
4) **How much do you need that particular cigarette:**

1 – Very Strongly Needed   2 – Strongly Needed   3 – Weakly Needed

# of Cigarette	Time	Food/Alcohol	Relaxation	Work	Social	Driving	Other (please describe)	Angry	Anxious	Bored	Depressed	Frustrated	Happy	Relaxed	Tired	Need Rating		
1																1	2	3
2																1	2	3
3																1	2	3
4																1	2	3
5																1	2	3
6																1	2	3
7																1	2	3
8																1	2	3
9																1	2	3
10																1	2	3
11																1	2	3
12																1	2	3
13																1	2	3
14																1	2	3
15																1	2	3
16																1	2	3
17																1	2	3
18																1	2	3
19																1	2	3
20																1	2	3

Assignment: Pack-Wraps

Wrap this daily cigarette count sheet around your pack of cigarettes and secure it with a rubber band. When you are about to take a cigarette, before you actually put it in your mouth and light up, indicate the following:

1) **Time of day**
2) **Activity you are involved in**
3) **Word/words that best describe your feeling at the time**
4) **How much do you need that particular cigarette:**

1 – Very Strongly Needed   **2 – Strongly Needed**   **3 – Weakly Needed**

# of Cigarette	Time	Food/Alcohol	Relaxation	Work	Social	Driving	Other (please describe)	Angry	Anxious	Bored	Depressed	Frustrated	Happy	Relaxed	Tired	Need Rating		
1																1	2	3
2																1	2	3
3																1	2	3
4																1	2	3
5																1	2	3
6																1	2	3
7																1	2	3
8																1	2	3
9																1	2	3
10																1	2	3
11																1	2	3
12																1	2	3
13																1	2	3
14																1	2	3
15																1	2	3
16																1	2	3
17																1	2	3
18																1	2	3
19																1	2	3
20																1	2	3

Assignment: Pack-Wraps

Wrap this daily cigarette count sheet around your pack of cigarettes and secure it with a rubber band. When you are about to take a cigarette, before you actually put it in your mouth and light up, indicate the following:

1) **Time of day**
2) **Activity you are involved in**
3) **Word/words that best describe your feeling at the time**
4) **How much do you need that particular cigarette:**

1 – Very Strongly Needed **2 – Strongly Needed** **3 – Weakly Needed**

# of Cigarette	Time	Food/Alcohol	Relaxation	Work	Social	Driving	Other (please describe)	Angry	Anxious	Bored	Depressed	Frustrated	Happy	Relaxed	Tired	Need Rating		
1																1	2	3
2																1	2	3
3																1	2	3
4																1	2	3
5																1	2	3
6																1	2	3
7																1	2	3
8																1	2	3
9																1	2	3
10																1	2	3
11																1	2	3
12																1	2	3
13																1	2	3
14																1	2	3
15																1	2	3
16																1	2	3
17																1	2	3
18																1	2	3
19																1	2	3
20																1	2	3

Assignment: Pack-Wraps

Wrap this daily cigarette count sheet around your pack of cigarettes and secure it with a rubber band. When you are about to take a cigarette, before you actually put it in your mouth and light up, indicate the following:

1) **Time of day**
2) **Activity you are involved in**
3) **Word/words that best describe your feeling at the time**
4) **How much do you need that particular cigarette:**

1 – Very Strongly Needed **2 – Strongly Needed** **3 – Weakly Needed**

# of Cigarette	Time	Food/Alcohol	Relaxation	Work	Social	Driving	Other (please describe)	Angry	Anxious	Bored	Depressed	Frustrated	Happy	Relaxed	Tired	Need Rating		
1																1	2	3
2																1	2	3
3																1	2	3
4																1	2	3
5																1	2	3
6																1	2	3
7																1	2	3
8																1	2	3
9																1	2	3
10																1	2	3
11																1	2	3
12																1	2	3
13																1	2	3
14																1	2	3
15																1	2	3
16																1	2	3
17																1	2	3
18																1	2	3
19																1	2	3
20																1	2	3

Assignment: Pack-Wraps

Wrap this daily cigarette count sheet around your pack of cigarettes and secure it with a rubber band. When you are about to take a cigarette, before you actually put it in your mouth and light up, indicate the following:

1) **Time of day**
2) **Activity you are involved in**
3) **Word/words that best describe your feeling at the time**
4) **How much do you need that particular cigarette:**

1 – Very Strongly Needed   2 – Strongly Needed   3 – Weakly Needed

# of Cigarette	Time	Food/Alcohol	Relaxation	Work	Social	Driving	Other (please describe)	Angry	Anxious	Bored	Depressed	Frustrated	Happy	Relaxed	Tired	Need Rating
1																1 2 3
2																1 2 3
3																1 2 3
4																1 2 3
5																1 2 3
6																1 2 3
7																1 2 3
8																1 2 3
9																1 2 3
10																1 2 3
11																1 2 3
12																1 2 3
13																1 2 3
14																1 2 3
15																1 2 3
16																1 2 3
17																1 2 3
18																1 2 3
19																1 2 3
20																1 2 3

Assignment: Pack-Wraps

Wrap this daily cigarette count sheet around your pack of cigarettes and secure it with a rubber band. When you are about to take a cigarette, before you actually put it in your mouth and light up, indicate the following:

1) **Time of day**
2) **Activity you are involved in**
3) **Word/words that best describe your feeling at the time**
4) **How much do you need that particular cigarette:**

1 – Very Strongly Needed   **2 – Strongly Needed**   **3 – Weakly Needed**

# of Cigarette	Time	Food/Alcohol	Relaxation	Work	Social	Driving	Other (please describe)	Angry	Anxious	Bored	Depressed	Frustrated	Happy	Relaxed	Tired	Need Rating
1																1 2 3
2																1 2 3
3																1 2 3
4																1 2 3
5																1 2 3
6																1 2 3
7																1 2 3
8																1 2 3
9																1 2 3
10																1 2 3
11																1 2 3
12																1 2 3
13																1 2 3
14																1 2 3
15																1 2 3
16																1 2 3
17																1 2 3
18																1 2 3
19																1 2 3
20																1 2 3

Assignment: Pack-Wraps

Wrap this daily cigarette count sheet around your pack of cigarettes and secure it with a rubber band. When you are about to take a cigarette, before you actually put it in your mouth and light up, indicate the following:

1) **Time of day**
2) **Activity you are involved in**
3) **Word/words that best describe your feeling at the time**
4) **How much do you need that particular cigarette:**

1 – **Very Strongly Needed**   2 – **Strongly Needed**   3 – **Weakly Needed**

# of Cigarette	Time	Food/Alcohol	Relaxation	Work	Social	Driving	Other (please describe)	Angry	Anxious	Bored	Depressed	Frustrated	Happy	Relaxed	Tired	Need Rating		
1																1	2	3
2																1	2	3
3																1	2	3
4																1	2	3
5																1	2	3
6																1	2	3
7																1	2	3
8																1	2	3
9																1	2	3
10																1	2	3
11																1	2	3
12																1	2	3
13																1	2	3
14																1	2	3
15																1	2	3
16																1	2	3
17																1	2	3
18																1	2	3
19																1	2	3
20																1	2	3

Assignment: Pack-Wraps

Wrap this daily cigarette count sheet around your pack of cigarettes and secure it with a rubber band. When you are about to take a cigarette, before you actually put it in your mouth and light up, indicate the following:

1) **Time of day**
2) **Activity you are involved in**
3) **Word/words that best describe your feeling at the time**
4) **How much do you need that particular cigarette:**

1 – **Very Strongly Needed**   2 – **Strongly Needed**   3 – **Weakly Needed**

# of Cigarette	Time	Food/Alcohol	Relaxation	Work	Social	Driving	Other (please describe)	Angry	Anxious	Bored	Depressed	Frustrated	Happy	Relaxed	Tired	Need Rating		
1																1	2	3
2																1	2	3
3																1	2	3
4																1	2	3
5																1	2	3
6																1	2	3
7																1	2	3
8																1	2	3
9																1	2	3
10																1	2	3
11																1	2	3
12																1	2	3
13																1	2	3
14																1	2	3
15																1	2	3
16																1	2	3
17																1	2	3
18																1	2	3
19																1	2	3
20																1	2	3

Assignment: Pack-Wraps

Wrap this daily cigarette count sheet around your pack of cigarettes and secure it with a rubber band. When you are about to take a cigarette, before you actually put it in your mouth and light up, indicate the following:

1) **Time of day**
2) **Activity you are involved in**
3) **Word/words that best describe your feeling at the time**
4) **How much do you need that particular cigarette:**

1 – Very Strongly Needed   **2 – Strongly Needed**   **3 – Weakly Needed**

# of Cigarette	Time	Food/Alcohol	Relaxation	Work	Social	Driving	Other (please describe)	Angry	Anxious	Bored	Depressed	Frustrated	Happy	Relaxed	Tired	Need Rating		
1																1	2	3
2																1	2	3
3																1	2	3
4																1	2	3
5																1	2	3
6																1	2	3
7																1	2	3
8																1	2	3
9																1	2	3
10																1	2	3
11																1	2	3
12																1	2	3
13																1	2	3
14																1	2	3
15																1	2	3
16																1	2	3
17																1	2	3
18																1	2	3
19																1	2	3
20																1	2	3

Assignment: Pack-Wraps

Wrap this daily cigarette count sheet around your pack of cigarettes and secure it with a rubber band. When you are about to take a cigarette, before you actually put it in your mouth and light up, indicate the following:

1) **Time of day**
2) **Activity you are involved in**
3) **Word/words that best describe your feeling at the time**
4) **How much do you need that particular cigarette:**

1 – **Very Strongly Needed**   2 – **Strongly Needed**   3 – **Weakly Needed**

# of Cigarette	Time	Food/Alcohol	Relaxation	Work	Social	Driving	Other (please describe)	Angry	Anxious	Bored	Depressed	Frustrated	Happy	Relaxed	Tired	Need Rating		
1																1	2	3
2																1	2	3
3																1	2	3
4																1	2	3
5																1	2	3
6																1	2	3
7																1	2	3
8																1	2	3
9																1	2	3
10																1	2	3
11																1	2	3
12																1	2	3
13																1	2	3
14																1	2	3
15																1	2	3
16																1	2	3
17																1	2	3
18																1	2	3
19																1	2	3
20																1	2	3

Assignment: Pack-Wraps

Wrap this daily cigarette count sheet around your pack of cigarettes and secure it with a rubber band. When you are about to take a cigarette, before you actually put it in your mouth and light up, indicate the following:

1) **Time of day**
2) **Activity you are involved in**
3) **Word/words that best describe your feeling at the time**
4) **How much do you need that particular cigarette:**

1 – **Very Strongly Needed**   2 – **Strongly Needed**   3 – **Weakly Needed**

# of Cigarette	Time	Food/Alcohol	Relaxation	Work	Social	Driving	Other (please describe)	Angry	Anxious	Bored	Depressed	Frustrated	Happy	Relaxed	Tired	Need Rating		
1																1	2	3
2																1	2	3
3																1	2	3
4																1	2	3
5																1	2	3
6																1	2	3
7																1	2	3
8																1	2	3
9																1	2	3
10																1	2	3
11																1	2	3
12																1	2	3
13																1	2	3
14																1	2	3
15																1	2	3
16																1	2	3
17																1	2	3
18																1	2	3
19																1	2	3
20																1	2	3

Assignment: Pack-Wraps

Wrap this daily cigarette count sheet around your pack of cigarettes and secure it with a rubber band. When you are about to take a cigarette, before you actually put it in your mouth and light up, indicate the following:

1) **Time of day**
2) **Activity you are involved in**
3) **Word/words that best describe your feeling at the time**
4) **How much do you need that particular cigarette:**

1 – Very Strongly Needed   **2 – Strongly Needed**   **3 – Weakly Needed**

# of Cigarette	Time	Food/Alcohol	Relaxation	Work	Social	Driving	Other (please describe)	Angry	Anxious	Bored	Depressed	Frustrated	Happy	Relaxed	Tired	Need Rating		
1																1	2	3
2																1	2	3
3																1	2	3
4																1	2	3
5																1	2	3
6																1	2	3
7																1	2	3
8																1	2	3
9																1	2	3
10																1	2	3
11																1	2	3
12																1	2	3
13																1	2	3
14																1	2	3
15																1	2	3
16																1	2	3
17																1	2	3
18																1	2	3
19																1	2	3
20																1	2	3

Assignment: Pack-Wraps

Wrap this daily cigarette count sheet around your pack of cigarettes and secure it with a rubber band. When you are about to take a cigarette, before you actually put it in your mouth and light up, indicate the following:

1) **Time of day**
2) **Activity you are involved in**
3) **Word/words that best describe your feeling at the time**
4) **How much do you need that particular cigarette:**

1 – Very Strongly Needed   **2 – Strongly Needed**   **3 – Weakly Needed**

# of Cigarette	Time	Food/Alcohol	Relaxation	Work	Social	Driving	Other (please describe)	Angry	Anxious	Bored	Depressed	Frustrated	Happy	Relaxed	Tired	Need Rating		
1																1	2	3
2																1	2	3
3																1	2	3
4																1	2	3
5																1	2	3
6																1	2	3
7																1	2	3
8																1	2	3
9																1	2	3
10																1	2	3
11																1	2	3
12																1	2	3
13																1	2	3
14																1	2	3
15																1	2	3
16																1	2	3
17																1	2	3
18																1	2	3
19																1	2	3
20																1	2	3

Assignment: Pack-Wraps

Wrap this daily cigarette count sheet around your pack of cigarettes and secure it with a rubber band. When you are about to take a cigarette, before you actually put it in your mouth and light up, indicate the following:

1) **Time of day**
2) **Activity you are involved in**
3) **Word/words that best describe your feeling at the time**
4) **How much do you need that particular cigarette:**

1 – Very Strongly Needed   **2 – Strongly Needed**   **3 – Weakly Needed**

# of Cigarette	Time	Food/Alcohol	Relaxation	Work	Social	Driving	Other (please describe)	Angry	Anxious	Bored	Depressed	Frustrated	Happy	Relaxed	Tired	Need Rating		
1																1	2	3
2																1	2	3
3																1	2	3
4																1	2	3
5																1	2	3
6																1	2	3
7																1	2	3
8																1	2	3
9																1	2	3
10																1	2	3
11																1	2	3
12																1	2	3
13																1	2	3
14																1	2	3
15																1	2	3
16																1	2	3
17																1	2	3
18																1	2	3
19																1	2	3
20																1	2	3

Assignment: Pack-Wraps

Wrap this daily cigarette count sheet around your pack of cigarettes and secure it with a rubber band. When you are about to take a cigarette, before you actually put it in your mouth and light up, indicate the following:

1) **Time of day**
2) **Activity you are involved in**
3) **Word/words that best describe your feeling at the time**
4) **How much do you need that particular cigarette:**

1 – Very Strongly Needed   **2 – Strongly Needed**   **3 – Weakly Needed**

# of Cigarette	Time	Food/Alcohol	Relaxation	Work	Social	Driving	Other (please describe)	Angry	Anxious	Bored	Depressed	Frustrated	Happy	Relaxed	Tired	Need Rating		
1																1	2	3
2																1	2	3
3																1	2	3
4																1	2	3
5																1	2	3
6																1	2	3
7																1	2	3
8																1	2	3
9																1	2	3
10																1	2	3
11																1	2	3
12																1	2	3
13																1	2	3
14																1	2	3
15																1	2	3
16																1	2	3
17																1	2	3
18																1	2	3
19																1	2	3
20																1	2	3

Assignment: Pack-Wraps

Wrap this daily cigarette count sheet around your pack of cigarettes and secure it with a rubber band. When you are about to take a cigarette, before you actually put it in your mouth and light up, indicate the following:

1) **Time of day**
2) **Activity you are involved in**
3) **Word/words that best describe your feeling at the time**
4) **How much do you need that particular cigarette:**

1 – Very Strongly Needed   **2 – Strongly Needed**   **3 – Weakly Needed**

# of Cigarette	Time	Food/Alcohol	Relaxation	Work	Social	Driving	Other (please describe)	Angry	Anxious	Bored	Depressed	Frustrated	Happy	Relaxed	Tired	Need Rating		
1																1	2	3
2																1	2	3
3																1	2	3
4																1	2	3
5																1	2	3
6																1	2	3
7																1	2	3
8																1	2	3
9																1	2	3
10																1	2	3
11																1	2	3
12																1	2	3
13																1	2	3
14																1	2	3
15																1	2	3
16																1	2	3
17																1	2	3
18																1	2	3
19																1	2	3
20																1	2	3

Assignment: Pack-Wraps

Wrap this daily cigarette count sheet around your pack of cigarettes and secure it with a rubber band. When you are about to take a cigarette, before you actually put it in your mouth and light up, indicate the following:

1) **Time of day**
2) **Activity you are involved in**
3) **Word/words that best describe your feeling at the time**
4) **How much do you need that particular cigarette:**

1 – Very Strongly Needed   2 – Strongly Needed   3 – Weakly Needed

# of Cigarette	Time	Food/Alcohol	Relaxation	Work	Social	Driving	Other (please describe)	Angry	Anxious	Bored	Depressed	Frustrated	Happy	Relaxed	Tired	Need Rating		
1																1	2	3
2																1	2	3
3																1	2	3
4																1	2	3
5																1	2	3
6																1	2	3
7																1	2	3
8																1	2	3
9																1	2	3
10																1	2	3
11																1	2	3
12																1	2	3
13																1	2	3
14																1	2	3
15																1	2	3
16																1	2	3
17																1	2	3
18																1	2	3
19																1	2	3
20																1	2	3

Assignment: Pack-Wraps

Wrap this daily cigarette count sheet around your pack of cigarettes and secure it with a rubber band. When you are about to take a cigarette, before you actually put it in your mouth and light up, indicate the following:

1) **Time of day**
2) **Activity you are involved in**
3) **Word/words that best describe your feeling at the time**
4) **How much do you need that particular cigarette:**

1 – **Very Strongly Needed**   2 – **Strongly Needed**   3 – **Weakly Needed**

# of Cigarette	Time	Food/Alcohol	Relaxation	Work	Social	Driving	Other (please describe)	Angry	Anxious	Bored	Depressed	Frustrated	Happy	Relaxed	Tired	Need Rating		
1																1	2	3
2																1	2	3
3																1	2	3
4																1	2	3
5																1	2	3
6																1	2	3
7																1	2	3
8																1	2	3
9																1	2	3
10																1	2	3
11																1	2	3
12																1	2	3
13																1	2	3
14																1	2	3
15																1	2	3
16																1	2	3
17																1	2	3
18																1	2	3
19																1	2	3
20																1	2	3

Assignment: Pack-Wraps

Wrap this daily cigarette count sheet around your pack of cigarettes and secure it with a rubber band. When you are about to take a cigarette, before you actually put it in your mouth and light up, indicate the following:

1) **Time of day**
2) **Activity you are involved in**
3) **Word/words that best describe your feeling at the time**
4) **How much do you need that particular cigarette:**

1 – **Very Strongly Needed**   2 – **Strongly Needed**   3 – **Weakly Needed**

# of Cigarette	Time	Food/Alcohol	Relaxation	Work	Social	Driving	Other (please describe)	Angry	Anxious	Bored	Depressed	Frustrated	Happy	Relaxed	Tired	Need Rating		
1																1	2	3
2																1	2	3
3																1	2	3
4																1	2	3
5																1	2	3
6																1	2	3
7																1	2	3
8																1	2	3
9																1	2	3
10																1	2	3
11																1	2	3
12																1	2	3
13																1	2	3
14																1	2	3
15																1	2	3
16																1	2	3
17																1	2	3
18																1	2	3
19																1	2	3
20																1	2	3

Assignment: Pack-Wraps

Wrap this daily cigarette count sheet around your pack of cigarettes and secure it with a rubber band. When you are about to take a cigarette, before you actually put it in your mouth and light up, indicate the following:

1) **Time of day**
2) **Activity you are involved in**
3) **Word/words that best describe your feeling at the time**
4) **How much do you need that particular cigarette:**

1 – Very Strongly Needed   2 – Strongly Needed   3 – Weakly Needed

# of Cigarette	Time	Food/Alcohol	Relaxation	Work	Social	Driving	Other (please describe)	Angry	Anxious	Bored	Depressed	Frustrated	Happy	Relaxed	Tired	Need Rating		
1																1	2	3
2																1	2	3
3																1	2	3
4																1	2	3
5																1	2	3
6																1	2	3
7																1	2	3
8																1	2	3
9																1	2	3
10																1	2	3
11																1	2	3
12																1	2	3
13																1	2	3
14																1	2	3
15																1	2	3
16																1	2	3
17																1	2	3
18																1	2	3
19																1	2	3
20																1	2	3

Assignment: Pack-Wraps

Wrap this daily cigarette count sheet around your pack of cigarettes and secure it with a rubber band. When you are about to take a cigarette, before you actually put it in your mouth and light up, indicate the following:

1) **Time of day**
2) **Activity you are involved in**
3) **Word/words that best describe your feeling at the time**
4) **How much do you need that particular cigarette:**

1 – **Very Strongly Needed**   2 – **Strongly Needed**   3 – **Weakly Needed**

# of Cigarette	Time	Food/Alcohol	Relaxation	Work	Social	Driving	Other (please describe)	Angry	Anxious	Bored	Depressed	Frustrated	Happy	Relaxed	Tired	Need Rating		
1																1	2	3
2																1	2	3
3																1	2	3
4																1	2	3
5																1	2	3
6																1	2	3
7																1	2	3
8																1	2	3
9																1	2	3
10																1	2	3
11																1	2	3
12																1	2	3
13																1	2	3
14																1	2	3
15																1	2	3
16																1	2	3
17																1	2	3
18																1	2	3
19																1	2	3
20																1	2	3

Assignment: Pack-Wraps

Wrap this daily cigarette count sheet around your pack of cigarettes and secure it with a rubber band. When you are about to take a cigarette, before you actually put it in your mouth and light up, indicate the following:

1) **Time of day**
2) **Activity you are involved in**
3) **Word/words that best describe your feeling at the time**
4) **How much do you need that particular cigarette:**

1 – Very Strongly Needed   2 – Strongly Needed   3 – Weakly Needed

# of Cigarette	Time	Food/Alcohol	Relaxation	Work	Social	Driving	Other (please describe)	Angry	Anxious	Bored	Depressed	Frustrated	Happy	Relaxed	Tired	Need Rating		
1																1	2	3
2																1	2	3
3																1	2	3
4																1	2	3
5																1	2	3
6																1	2	3
7																1	2	3
8																1	2	3
9																1	2	3
10																1	2	3
11																1	2	3
12																1	2	3
13																1	2	3
14																1	2	3
15																1	2	3
16																1	2	3
17																1	2	3
18																1	2	3
19																1	2	3
20																1	2	3

Assignment: Pack-Wraps

Wrap this daily cigarette count sheet around your pack of cigarettes and secure it with a rubber band. When you are about to take a cigarette, before you actually put it in your mouth and light up, indicate the following:

1) **Time of day**
2) **Activity you are involved in**
3) **Word/words that best describe your feeling at the time**
4) **How much do you need that particular cigarette:**

1 – **Very Strongly Needed**   2 – **Strongly Needed**   3 – **Weakly Needed**

# of Cigarette	Time	Food/Alcohol	Relaxation	Work	Social	Driving	Other (please describe)	Angry	Anxious	Bored	Depressed	Frustrated	Happy	Relaxed	Tired	Need Rating		
1																1	2	3
2																1	2	3
3																1	2	3
4																1	2	3
5																1	2	3
6																1	2	3
7																1	2	3
8																1	2	3
9																1	2	3
10																1	2	3
11																1	2	3
12																1	2	3
13																1	2	3
14																1	2	3
15																1	2	3
16																1	2	3
17																1	2	3
18																1	2	3
19																1	2	3
20																1	2	3

Assignment: Pack-Wraps

Wrap this daily cigarette count sheet around your pack of cigarettes and secure it with a rubber band. When you are about to take a cigarette, before you actually put it in your mouth and light up, indicate the following:

1) **Time of day**
2) **Activity you are involved in**
3) **Word/words that best describe your feeling at the time**
4) **How much do you need that particular cigarette:**

1 – Very Strongly Needed   2 – Strongly Needed   3 – Weakly Needed

# of Cigarette	Time	Food/Alcohol	Relaxation	Work	Social	Driving	Other (please describe)	Angry	Anxious	Bored	Depressed	Frustrated	Happy	Relaxed	Tired	Need Rating		
1																1	2	3
2																1	2	3
3																1	2	3
4																1	2	3
5																1	2	3
6																1	2	3
7																1	2	3
8																1	2	3
9																1	2	3
10																1	2	3
11																1	2	3
12																1	2	3
13																1	2	3
14																1	2	3
15																1	2	3
16																1	2	3
17																1	2	3
18																1	2	3
19																1	2	3
20																1	2	3

Assignment: Pack-Wraps

Wrap this daily cigarette count sheet around your pack of cigarettes and secure it with a rubber band. When you are about to take a cigarette, before you actually put it in your mouth and light up, indicate the following:

1) **Time of day**
2) **Activity you are involved in**
3) **Word/words that best describe your feeling at the time**
4) **How much do you need that particular cigarette:**

1 – Very Strongly Needed   **2 – Strongly Needed**   **3 – Weakly Needed**

# of Cigarette	Time	Food/Alcohol	Relaxation	Work	Social	Driving	Other (please describe)	Angry	Anxious	Bored	Depressed	Frustrated	Happy	Relaxed	Tired	Need Rating
1																1 2 3
2																1 2 3
3																1 2 3
4																1 2 3
5																1 2 3
6																1 2 3
7																1 2 3
8																1 2 3
9																1 2 3
10																1 2 3
11																1 2 3
12																1 2 3
13																1 2 3
14																1 2 3
15																1 2 3
16																1 2 3
17																1 2 3
18																1 2 3
19																1 2 3
20																1 2 3

Assignment: Pack-Wraps

Wrap this daily cigarette count sheet around your pack of cigarettes and secure it with a rubber band. When you are about to take a cigarette, before you actually put it in your mouth and light up, indicate the following:

1) **Time of day**
2) **Activity you are involved in**
3) **Word/words that best describe your feeling at the time**
4) **How much do you need that particular cigarette:**

1 – Very Strongly Needed   **2 – Strongly Needed**   **3 – Weakly Needed**

# of Cigarette	Time	Food/Alcohol	Relaxation	Work	Social	Driving	Other (please describe)	Angry	Anxious	Bored	Depressed	Frustrated	Happy	Relaxed	Tired	Need Rating		
1																1	2	3
2																1	2	3
3																1	2	3
4																1	2	3
5																1	2	3
6																1	2	3
7																1	2	3
8																1	2	3
9																1	2	3
10																1	2	3
11																1	2	3
12																1	2	3
13																1	2	3
14																1	2	3
15																1	2	3
16																1	2	3
17																1	2	3
18																1	2	3
19																1	2	3
20																1	2	3

Assignment: Pack-Wraps

Wrap this daily cigarette count sheet around your pack of cigarettes and secure it with a rubber band. When you are about to take a cigarette, before you actually put it in your mouth and light up, indicate the following:

1) **Time of day**
2) **Activity you are involved in**
3) **Word/words that best describe your feeling at the time**
4) **How much do you need that particular cigarette:**

1 – Very Strongly Needed   **2 – Strongly Needed**   **3 – Weakly Needed**

# of Cigarette	Time	Food/Alcohol	Relaxation	Work	Social	Driving	Other (please describe)	Angry	Anxious	Bored	Depressed	Frustrated	Happy	Relaxed	Tired	Need Rating		
1																1	2	3
2																1	2	3
3																1	2	3
4																1	2	3
5																1	2	3
6																1	2	3
7																1	2	3
8																1	2	3
9																1	2	3
10																1	2	3
11																1	2	3
12																1	2	3
13																1	2	3
14																1	2	3
15																1	2	3
16																1	2	3
17																1	2	3
18																1	2	3
19																1	2	3
20																1	2	3

Assignment: Pack-Wraps

Wrap this daily cigarette count sheet around your pack of cigarettes and secure it with a rubber band. When you are about to take a cigarette, before you actually put it in your mouth and light up, indicate the following:

1) **Time of day**
2) **Activity you are involved in**
3) **Word/words that best describe your feeling at the time**
4) **How much do you need that particular cigarette:**

1 – Very Strongly Needed   **2 – Strongly Needed**   **3 – Weakly Needed**

# of Cigarette	Time	Food/Alcohol	Relaxation	Work	Social	Driving	Other (please describe)	Angry	Anxious	Bored	Depressed	Frustrated	Happy	Relaxed	Tired	Need Rating
1																1 2 3
2																1 2 3
3																1 2 3
4																1 2 3
5																1 2 3
6																1 2 3
7																1 2 3
8																1 2 3
9																1 2 3
10																1 2 3
11																1 2 3
12																1 2 3
13																1 2 3
14																1 2 3
15																1 2 3
16																1 2 3
17																1 2 3
18																1 2 3
19																1 2 3
20																1 2 3

Assignment: Pack-Wraps

Wrap this daily cigarette count sheet around your pack of cigarettes and secure it with a rubber band. When you are about to take a cigarette, before you actually put it in your mouth and light up, indicate the following:

1) **Time of day**
2) **Activity you are involved in**
3) **Word/words that best describe your feeling at the time**
4) **How much do you need that particular cigarette:**

1 – **Very Strongly Needed**   2 – **Strongly Needed**   3 – **Weakly Needed**

# of Cigarette	Time	Food/Alcohol	Relaxation	Work	Social	Driving	Other (please describe)	Angry	Anxious	Bored	Depressed	Frustrated	Happy	Relaxed	Tired	Need Rating		
1																1	2	3
2																1	2	3
3																1	2	3
4																1	2	3
5																1	2	3
6																1	2	3
7																1	2	3
8																1	2	3
9																1	2	3
10																1	2	3
11																1	2	3
12																1	2	3
13																1	2	3
14																1	2	3
15																1	2	3
16																1	2	3
17																1	2	3
18																1	2	3
19																1	2	3
20																1	2	3

Assignment: Pack-Wraps

Wrap this daily cigarette count sheet around your pack of cigarettes and secure it with a rubber band. When you are about to take a cigarette, before you actually put it in your mouth and light up, indicate the following:

1) **Time of day**
2) **Activity you are involved in**
3) **Word/words that best describe your feeling at the time**
4) **How much do you need that particular cigarette:**

1 – Very Strongly Needed   **2 – Strongly Needed**   **3 – Weakly Needed**

# of Cigarette	Time	Food/Alcohol	Relaxation	Work	Social	Driving	Other (please describe)	Angry	Anxious	Bored	Depressed	Frustrated	Happy	Relaxed	Tired	Need Rating		
1																1	2	3
2																1	2	3
3																1	2	3
4																1	2	3
5																1	2	3
6																1	2	3
7																1	2	3
8																1	2	3
9																1	2	3
10																1	2	3
11																1	2	3
12																1	2	3
13																1	2	3
14																1	2	3
15																1	2	3
16																1	2	3
17																1	2	3
18																1	2	3
19																1	2	3
20																1	2	3

Daily Diary

Day	No. of Cigarettes Smoked	Activity (type and minutes)	Meals or Snacks Calories Consumed	Alcohol Intake
Mon				
Tue				
Wed				
Thurs				
Fri				
Sat				
Sun				

Daily Diary

Day	No. of Cigarettes Smoked	Activity (type and minutes)	Meals or Snacks Calories Consumed	Alcohol Intake
Mon				
Tue				
Wed				
Thurs				
Fri				
Sat				
Sun				

Daily Diary

Day	No. of Cigarettes Smoked	Activity (type and minutes)	Meals or Snacks Calories Consumed	Alcohol Intake
Mon				
Tue				
Wed				
Thurs				
Fri				
Sat				
Sun				

Daily Diary

Day	No. of Cigarettes Smoked	Activity (type and minutes)	Meals or Snacks Calories Consumed	Alcohol Intake
Mon				
Tue				
Wed				
Thurs				
Fri				
Sat				
Sun				

Daily Diary

Day	No. of Cigarettes Smoked	Activity (type and minutes)	Meals or Snacks Calories Consumed	Alcohol Intake
Mon				
Tue				
Wed				
Thurs				
Fri				
Sat				
Sun				

Daily Diary

Day	No. of Cigarettes Smoked	Activity (type and minutes)	Meals or Snacks Calories Consumed	Alcohol Intake
Mon				
Tue				
Wed				
Thurs				
Fri				
Sat				
Sun				

Daily Diary

Day	No. of Cigarettes Smoked	Activity (type and minutes)	Meals or Snacks Calories Consumed	Alcohol Intake
Mon				
Tue				
Wed				
Thurs				
Fri				
Sat				
Sun				

Daily Diary

Day	No. of Cigarettes Smoked	Activity (type and minutes)	Meals or Snacks Calories Consumed	Alcohol Intake
Mon				
Tue				
Wed				
Thurs				
Fri				
Sat				
Sun				

Daily Diary

Day	No. of Cigarettes Smoked	Activity (type and minutes)	Meals or Snacks Calories Consumed	Alcohol Intake
Mon				
Tue				
Wed				
Thurs				
Fri				
Sat				
Sun				

Daily Diary

Day	No. of Cigarettes Smoked	Activity (type and minutes)	Meals or Snacks Calories Consumed	Alcohol Intake
Mon				
Tue				
Wed				
Thurs				
Fri				
Sat				
Sun				